The Legacy Renewed

Football and Foreman Field: Norfolk Division – Old Dominion University

Peter C. Stewart
Thomas R. Garrett

Outer Banks Press

The Legacy Renewed

Football and Foreman Field: Norfolk Division—Old Dominion University

Peter C. Stewart and Thomas R. Garrett

First edition
Published in 2009 by Outer Banks Press, a subsidiary of OBBC, Inc.

ISBN: 978-0-9778924-3-3

Library of Congress Cataloguing-in-Publication data available by request

Editor: Jim Ducibella
Design: Linda L. Lauby, Outer Banks Press

Printed in China

Cover Images: Courtesy of Sargeant Memorial Room, Norfolk Public Library

Outer Banks Press
Post Office Box 2829
Kitty Hawk, North Carolina 27949
252.261.0612
mail@outerbankspress.com
www.outerbankspress.com

TO THE DIVISION PLAYERS

WHO GAVE THEIR LIVES IN SERVICE TO THEIR COUNTRY.

Wilson Dozier

David A. Dozier

Adrian Dorsey Cooper

Carl Hull

Richard James

Albert Roy Kaufmann

Herbert Moore

On September 5, 1930 the old Larchmont Elementary School would open its doors to 206 students of what would eventually become Old Dominion University. (Courtesy of Special Collections and University Archives, Perry Library, Old Dominion University)

Contents

Foreword

Beginning September 5, 2009, life at Old Dominion University will never be the same. Think about that statement. ODU, my alma mater, was founded 79 years ago. During that time, it has been governed by many capable administrators. Older buildings have been razed and many newer, better-equipped buildings have replaced them or have been added to the landscape.

Our university has featured many outstanding professors and programs. Thousands of students have graduated and forged their paths in all walks of life—even broadcasting. For all of that inspired leadership, campus growth and graduation power, how many events have transpired that created a fundamental change in life at the university? I don't know the answer and, in fact, any answer is open to debate. Except one: football.

The day I picked up a copy of *The New York Times* and saw there was a story on football at ODU, I knew Old Dominion would never be the same once Bobby Wilder and his team ran onto the field. *The New York Times* was so captivated by happenings on Hampton Boulevard, hundreds of miles from Times Square, that they devoted a healthy number of precious column inches to Monarch football. Did I mention that this occurred more than a year before opening day?

It's stating the obvious, but so much will be different from the manner in which ODU played football 58 years ago—the focus of this fine publication—and the way it will be played from here on out.

I'll bet throughout this season, and many seasons to come, hundreds of alumni who might never take the time to return to campus will flock back to ODU and Foreman Field to see a game. That's if they can score a seat; after all, it is the hottest ticket in town! They'll visit the Webb Center, stroll through the University Village for some coffee or a slice of pizza, gawk at the new student recreation center and marvel at how lucky today's ODU students are. I've done that on visits back and that's pre-football.

With football, the acrid smell of charcoal will fill the air, and shouts of "watch out!"

will reverberate off the walls as embarrassed tailgaters toss footballs in directions far from where they were aiming. The stadium lights will come on and the Monarch Marching Band will parade through campus, gathering fans for a pilgrimage to Foreman Field. Week after week, year after year, new students, new alumni and new players will join with long-time supporters in a ritual that will never get stale.

Had someone suggested anything like this in 1987, when I graduated from ODU, his or her sanity would have been questioned. Many of us tried to bring football back. I guess the timing just wasn't right. So Old Dominion students watched *other* colleges and universities, and even partied in *other* schools' parking lots and student unions. Likely, they rarely gave their school a thought from the time they pulled out of the parking lot on Friday afternoon until the time they hurried back for Monday's classes. They worked near home, played near home, and slept in beds at home. There was a sense of detachment from the university that men's and women's basketball only helped bridge.

Not anymore. In some respects, Old Dominion becomes a *real* university on September 5; not just a place for the important work of becoming well-educated and prepared for what's down the road. But it becomes a social universe to thousands, where past, present and future Monarchs congregate, celebrate and, only occasionally I hope, commiserate with each other, side-by-side, arm-in-arm, bumper-by-bumper. Life at ODU will never be the same. Count on it. Now quick, somebody hand me a Monarch Burger and a drink. I hope no one is sitting in my seat. It's almost time for kickoff.

Jay Harris
ESPN SportsCenter Anchor
ODU Class of 1987

Acknowledgments

Among those who helped with the creation of this study, Troy Valos of the Sargeant Memorial Room, Norfolk Public Library did enough work in gathering photographs and following leads that he qualifies as a third author. We also thank Robert Hitchings, the enthusiastic head of the local research room. Sonia Yaco and Harry "Mel" Frizzell III, at the Old Dominion University Archives helped immeasurably, as did Mona Farrow and the staff in the microfilm room at the University. Also helpful were folks at the Reynolds Library at Wake Forest and at the College of William & Mary's Swem Library. Others at Old Dominion who rendered assistance were Dr. James Jarrett, athletic director; Tina Price, director of publications/creative services; Debbie White, senior associate athletic director; Bobby Wilder, head football coach; Carol Hudson, sports information director; and Kimberly Zivkovich, associate sports information director. We appreciate Rhetta Wilson and Elaine Dawson for assisting with the writing and preparation of the text. A special thanks to Linda Lauby of Outer Banks Press for helping to make this book a reality. We also wish to thank Jim Ducibella, retired sports writer for *The Virginian-Pilot*, who gave invaluable guidance, especially in arranging contacts and in editing the text, and Jay Harris, anchor of *ESPN SportsCenter*, for the fine foreword.

Several former players provided their time and recollections to help with the project —Rhea Walker, the oldest, played on teams between 1932 and 1934. John Brown, Bill Brichter, and Bill Baker participated in the late 1930s. All of them related wonderful stories about their experiences. Only the authors are accountable for any errors.

Most of the photographs came from the collection now housed at the Sargeant Memorial Room at the Norfolk Public Library. These were the work of Charles Borjes of Norfolk's *The Virginian-Pilot*, the morning daily, and Harden D. Vollmer of *The Ledger-Dispatch*, the afternoon daily. Some of the photos were used by permission from the Old Dominion University Perry Library archives.

Preface

With Old Dominion University about to restart its football program after an absence of almost 70 years, it seems like a good time to peruse the history of football in the Norfolk area. This labor of love, however, turned out to be more complicated than we originally thought. Something needs to be said about our method of research. We combed numerous microfilm files of Norfolk's newspapers, *The Virginian-Pilot* and *The Ledger-Dispatch*. In addition, game accounts and other information could also be found in the Norfolk Division campus newspaper, *The High Hat* and to a lesser extent in *The Flat Hat* at the College of William & Mary, the parent institution. From these sources, we were able to create a unified roster, found in the book's appendix, covering the 11 years of football for the Division, but only an excessive optimist can believe this list is completely accurate. Every season started with a varying number of participants, ranging from 12 to 50. Some would stop coming to practice, and others never heard of before would surface. Some would show up for a team photo but never be mentioned in any game accounts. In addition, reporters often changed the spelling of names or even the names themselves. We have done our best to reconcile these differences.

In Appendix I, an "m" stands for monogram (denoting recipients of football letters), but the campus press published these lists only for a few years. Some of those playing for three years, like Rhea Walker, also received a gold football charm at the end of their third season. Although we tried hard not to exclude anyone that merited inclusion on the roster, we doubtless included some who were never on the team and left out others who were but never had their names divulged. Those who follow up our leads will probably discover important omissions.

One would think that the Norfolk Division won-lost record would be pretty much factual, but it is anything but. Some say the overall record was 68 wins, 27 losses, and 5 ties. As compiled from accounts in all the newspapers, the record was 48 wins, 36 losses and 5 ties, quite a different set of numbers. It is possible that the newspapers did not report all the games and it is also conceivable that we missed an account or two. But the Division had too many gaps in the schedule to have possibly played 100 games over 11 seasons. Moreover, some of the games given press coverage were really "exhibitions," not intended to count. Why such a discrepancy exists about wins and losses remains a mystery.

P.S. As we were about to go to press, the ODU Board of Visitors announced that the football facility would carry the name "S. B. Ballard Stadium at Foreman Field."

CHAPTER ONE

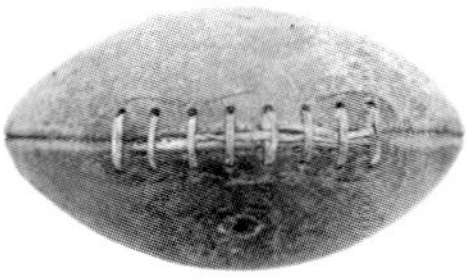

The Early Years

American-style football first appeared at Yale and other elite northeastern colleges in the early 1880s and spread across the land, being picked up first by other colleges and then spreading to the rest of the population. It was a rough game that evolved out of the English sport of rugby. In the early 1880s Yale alumnus Walter Camp, "the Father of Football," introduced the use of downs and a scrimmage line, and once tackling and blocking below the waist were permitted, it settled down to be largely a defensive battle. Teams resorted to wedge plays, and for a time in the 1890s something called the "flying wedge," usually used after a punt or a kickoff. Students at the University of Virginia picked up the game, largely from Princeton, toward the end of the 1880s.

The first Virginia institution of higher learning to play a contest in the Hampton Roads area was probably Richmond College (now the University of Richmond), which, according to legend, lost to Norfolk Academy in the early 1890s. The Richmond school also played a series of three games against the Norfolk YMCA in 1893. The Y, composed to some extent of ex-collegians, defeated the College of William & Mary (the first football team at the school) the same year at a field in Ghent. At most, a few hundred people, including young women, attended these affairs, mostly friends and family of the participants. The independent club from Hampton easily defeated the University of North Carolina and tied the University of Virginia later in the so-called "Gay Nineties." In 1900, the University of Maryland bested the Portsmouth Athletics, an independent club, 12-6.[1]

Hampton Normal and Agricultural Institute, a private college for African Americans, which additionally had a large contingent of Native Americans, put on games early in the 20th century. Old Point Comfort College, a Roman Catholic institution close to Fort Monroe, also fielded teams and once played the Native Americans from Hampton Normal and Agricultural Institute. An artillery school at Fort Monroe had teams that sometimes played on the grounds inside the moat.

Although collegians had occasionally forayed into the area before the turn of the century, the first major collegiate game in Norfolk occurred on a late-November Saturday in 1900, pitting the University of Virginia against the University of North Carolina at League Park, located a block or two east of Church Street on Princess Anne Road. A reporter with *The Virginian-Pilot* expected a hard-fought, close struggle, and betting seemed unusually heavy, as gamblers assessed the performance of each club against common adversaries. Norfolk's business community expressed considerable pleasure that its city hosted the contest, having lured it away from the state capital. The local newspaper editor welcomed the "young gentlemen" from the two universities as well as their supporters, but warned spectators not to let their enthusiasm "sweep them out on the field and in the way of the players."[2]

The night before the game, the lobby of the newly built Monticello Hotel reverberated with yelling and singing, as Norfolk's elite watched from the balcony. Even though a recent fire disrupted trolley service to the game, the momentous event went off without a hitch. Virginia's Orange and Blue won, 17-0, in a game that supposedly determined the championship of the South before "fully" 6,000 fans, almost equally divided in their support, if colors were any indication. The morning daily contained plenty of sketches, including those of young ladies in full fashion and of each starting player, along with an account of the contest. Afterward, the alumni of both universities sponsored a "brilliant" reception at the Norfolk Country Club, located near what is now the western edge of the Old Dominion University campus next to the Elizabeth River. The club's 9-hole golf course stood nearby, only a few yards from one recently built on top of what was once a huge dump. Participants, including both teams, came by trolley and then took carriages down a well-lighted path right across what is now the main part of the ODU campus.[3]

The next year (1901), the University of Virginia Cavaliers and North Carolinians returned to League Park to battle amid similar hoopla. The Carolinians made The Monticello Hotel their headquarters while the University of Virginia contingent stayed at the rebuilt Atlantic Hotel. During the contest Carolina, undefeated against a weak schedule, lost to the Virginians, 33-0, before 7,000 spectators.

Next came the first battle between Virginia Military Institute and Virginia Tech played in Norfolk. On Thanksgiving Day, the latter eased by the former, 21-0, before 5,000 fans, as two backs named Carpenter and Counselman consistently broke through the VMI Keydet line, carrying their eleven to what the reporter considered the Southern championship that year.[4]

In 1902, the University of North Carolina and the Blue and Gray of Georgetown inaugurated play at Lafayette Field, located on Church Street, immediately north and east of the railroad tracks terminating at the Lamberts Point coal piers. Theater owner and manager Otto Wells gave both clubs tickets to the play "Fiddle-Dee-Dee" at his Granby Theater the evening after the game. With the stores in downtown Norfolk draped in combinations of blue and white, and blue and gray, and chrysanthemums of every hue filling every empty space, 5,000 fans made their way to Lafayette Field, which held more seats than League Park. The first encounter became somewhat tarnished when seven "sporting characters" sold 1,000 bogus tickets, causing confusion at game time, the perpetrators being prosecuted for "felonious conspiracy to commit grand larceny." Using "incessant plunges," with an occasional end run, the Hoyas won, 12-5, in a cleanly played contest.[5]

Also that year, as Norfolk enhanced its reputation as a center for football, the University of Virginia took on the famed Carlisle Indian Industrial School's team (from Pennsylvania) at Lafayette Field. The "Red-Skinned Warriors" were favored in the betting, either 5-2 or 2-1, with bets ranging as high as $1,000 (when the average working man made about half that for a year's work). Some 6,000 fans thoroughly enjoyed a Virginia upset attained when, with the score, 6-5, Carlisle's extra-point drop-kick attempt struck the goal post. That fall, Tech and the Keydets returned to Norfolk to continue their rivalry, only to have Tech's Blacksburg boys win again by an even more lopsided margin, 50-5, as the great Hunter Carpenter led the way.[6]

The next year (1903) brought five collegiate contests involving seven different institutions of higher learning to Norfolk. Georgetown, coached by C. M. Barry, a recent graduate of the Washington, D.C. school who had earlier attended St. Mary's in Norfolk, again played the University of North Carolina in early October, with the Georgetown Hoyas reversing the result, winning 33-0. But only 2,000 fans braved icy weather to take in the contest. About the same number watched Richmond College subdue Hampden-Sydney to set the stage for an expected "fierce" match between UNC and Virginia Polytechnic Institute. The "sporting fraternity" could not really determine which eleven should be favored, but the boys from Blacksburg, with the "marvelous right halfback" Carpenter running through the opposition, easily won by three touchdowns. Now with three collegiate contests already played, the largest crowd to date (6,000) showed up to watch Captain Branch Johnson from Norfolk and the Cavaliers battle to a tie, 6-6, versus Carlisle, the famed Indian school. On Thanksgiving Day, the local Norfolk independent club, which contained some ex-collegians, overcame the University of Maryland, but only 500 spectators took advantage of the presentation.[7]

In early November of 1904 Georgetown "shattered" the University of North Carolina, which had the "Wizard of the Gridiron," Hunter Carpenter, who after playing several seasons for VPI, moved to Chapel Hill, North Carolina. Despite his best efforts, North Carolina gave way to the Hoyas, 16-0. Carpenter jokingly flung the oval into the stands after the game, an act considered poor sportsmanship. The next year (1905) the University of Virginia put in an appearance at Lafayette Field before some 3,500, and with "superior end plays" and "clever sprinting" offset Bucknell University's exclusive use of "tandem plays," 15-11. Very likely the most well-attended game of this era took place on Thanksgiving 1905, when some 12,000 crowded into Lafayette Field, many standing on the sidelines, to watch the Blue and White from North Carolina subdue the Cavaliers, 17-0. The local press believed that the number of spectators exceeded any contest ever played in Dixie. That attendance proved to be the high-water mark of old-style football in Norfolk.[8]

After North Carolina lost to Virginia, 12-11, in 1904, Carpenter transferred back to VPI to have another crack at the Cavaliers in 1905, despite protests from many Virginia fans, including those from the Norfolk and Portsmouth Alumni Association over his alleged professionalism. In that disputed game in Richmond, VPI triumphed handily, although the great back was ejected from the game when he ended a play by knocking out a Cavalier player who had been slugging him with his fists as Carpenter carried him for ample yardage. Disturbed by the loss and the circumstances surrounding it, the university would not play VPI again until 1923.[9]

The fundamental nature of the game would start changing the next year. Collegiate officials (what later came to be called the National Collegiate Athletic Association), imbued with the progressive spirit that stressed order in business affairs as well as in American social life, introduced the forward pass, although in a restricted fashion. They treated incomplete passes as either fumbles or at times as a violation requiring a yardage penalty. The pass could only travel five yards either side of center. Over the next six years (1906-1912), several rule changes forced teams to keep seven players on the line, not use forward motion plays, and to move the ball at least 10 yards in 4 downs, rather than 5 in 3. Rule changes between 1910 and 1912 reduced the length of the field from 110 to 100 yards, had kickoffs from the 40- rather than the 50-yard line, abolished the onside kick, allowed the forward pass to score a touchdown (which also necessitated installing end zones), and increased the value of a touchdown from 5 to 6 points (an earlier change demoted the value of a field goal to 3 points). Officials also changed the shape of the football by tapering the ends, thus making it easier to pass but more difficult to drop kick. In the mid-1930s the football became even thinner.[10]

Because the new plays were designed to make the game more exciting for spectators as well as save players from injury or death, it seems unlikely that the subsequent decline of interest in collegiate football in Norfolk could be due to these changes. What did prevent the sport from rising in popularity was the inability of local businessmen to attract high quality collegiate clubs. This failure also may have been due to a de-emphasis on football at some of the state's colleges, especially at the University of Virginia, where the faculty took a greater role in athletics and President Edwin A. Alderman, once a strong promoter of the sport, modified his views. The death of Cavalier halfback Archer Christian in 1909, while playing against Georgetown in Washington, D.C. coincides with the decline and with many of the rule changes already mentioned. Ironically, the game eventually became safer when players started wearing leather helmets, which did not require any specific alterations of rules until 1939. Norfolk and Portsmouth graduates of the University of

Virginia voted on whether to give up football, with younger alums familiar with the game outvoting the more elderly grads. Even though they voted to keep a football program, school officials put more restraints on the student football association.[11]

During the years of transition, interest in collegiate football in the Norfolk area remained on a level below that attained in the Thanksgiving 1905 contest. In 1906, Bucknell bested VPI, 10-0, with an audience of 4,000. When an official called back an apparent Tech touchdown because of a holding call, allowing Bucknell to score a second touchdown on the ensuing play (on a wayward punt after he had blown his whistle before the play started), a mob of Tech supporters chased a referee across the field of play. It turned out the referee chased by the mob had not been the one who had made the calls.

That year Carlisle eked out an 18-17 win over the Cavaliers on Thanksgiving Day in the "most spectacular gridiron battle ever waged on a Southern field," according to the reporter for *The Virginian-Pilot*. It would be hard to find any more exciting or more "fierce" football than that played by these two teams over the years. Carlisle was widely considered to be in the top level of collegiate football. The coach for Carlisle in 1906 was the famous Glenn "Pop" Warner.[12]

For the next several years, interest in college football in the area fluctuated but eventually waned, particularly as the second decade of the century advanced. In early November 1907, during the time of the exposition in honor of the Jamestown settlement held at what is now Naval Station Norfolk, the Cavaliers returned to Norfolk to lose to powerful Sewanee (the University of the South), 12-0, at Lafayette Field. They also lost to North Carolina A&M (now North Carolina State), 10-4 (the loser's points resulting from a field goal), on Thanksgiving that year. (The game took place before the 3-point rule change.)

On Thanksgiving Day 1908 at Lafayette Field some 4,000 watched North Carolina A&M slip by Virginia Tech, 6-5, the "fiercest and closest contest" ever played on the field, according to the press. The Virginia school's only loss before then came at the hands of Navy. Earlier that season, "thousands" watched the Cavaliers overcome the Aggies of North Carolina A&M. Eleven thousand came out on Thanksgiving in 1909 to see Coach Branch Bocock guide his Blacksburg boys to a solid win over the Aggies at the new League Park, located on the south side of 18th Street just east of Granby (later the location of the trolley car barn). The principal owner of the park was Otto Wells, who also owned the

Ocean View Amusement Park. In 1910, some 10,000 watched Davis Robertson (from Portsmouth) and the North Carolina Aggies run against VPI at Lafayette Field on Thanksgiving. The UNC-Virginia match-up that day in Richmond, however, drew some 15,000, hinting that Norfolk had lost its place in the football sun.[13]

Earlier that November in 1910, Washington and Lee of Lexington, Virginia, defeated UNC in Norfolk, with photographs clearly showing many empty seats in the bleachers on both sides of the field.

A 1911 match-up between Tech and A&M disturbed lots of folks because of the poor trolley service but is chiefly remembered for the big argument between the two colleges over whether Davis Robertson should be barred from college sports because he had played as a professional. He had played for a professional baseball team in Elizabeth City, North Carolina the previous summer, although he claimed not to have been paid to play. Under pressure, Tech agreed to go on with the scheduled game, but declared an end to the series. Because of a football injury, Robertson lost his chance to reach the major leagues as a pitcher, but John McGraw of the New York Giants converted him to an outfielder, where he played in the 1917 World Series.

In 1912, Washington and Lee again proved to have the best college eleven in the Virginia-North Carolina region when it defeated A&M in the rain, with barely 3,000 watching at Lafayette Field. In 1913, A&M ruined Washington and Lee's bid to win the Mid-Atlantic championship, 6-0, at still another League Park, this one located a block or two north of the previous one on 18th Street, diagonally across the railroad tracks and southwest of city-owned Lafayette Field, which would be abandoned as a stadium site until 1940. Unlike Lafayette Field, this new "league park," like the others with that name, was principally a baseball field, but it had peculiar dimensions. The owners at the time, who happened to be residents of Roanoke, planned for a spacious facility, but halfway into the project, they discovered the existence of a paper street (a road or street that appears on maps but does not exist in reality) cutting diagonally across left field. That legal snag meant the baseball field's left-field corner ended up being about 235 feet from home plate. One can only wonder how the owners were able to cram a football field into this setting. Over the winter the city council removed the paper street, thus allowing the owners to move the left-field fence closer to the railroad tracks and providing ample room for football.[14]

In 1914, the Generals got revenge, winning 7-0, before 5,000 in an exciting contest at a larger League Park. That year, the University of Virginia's Norfolk and Portsmouth alumni association resolved to ask the university to renew its games in Norfolk, but nothing came of this idea. The next year, the local press expressed discontent about Norfolk having been the site for only one major college game over the past three or four years. "More Football Games Sought for Norfolk," the headline noted, with the article explaining that the Norfolk Chamber of Commerce was in the process of negotiating with managers of the leading clubs in Virginia and North Carolina for games. The article attributed the recent weak attendance to competition with Thoroughbred horse racing north of Norfolk. Starting in 1907, near the Jamestown Exposition, these races usually took place in April and November and consumed six days a week each month. However, they ceased in April 1914 when Governor Henry Stuart hired rifle-wielding detectives from the Roanoke area to arrest gamblers, which, in effect, forced closure of the track. Failure to provide contests in the fall of 1914, therefore, was due to the inability to come to terms about renting League Park from its new owner, a local resident. With that matter resolved, the chamber hoped to schedule games between major university rivals. In its single experience with such teams that year, Norfolk's fans watched Washington and Lee pummel the Aggies, 48-13, to give the winners the lead in the South Atlantic championship.[15]

But the next year, instead of the several possible games mentioned, Norfolk drew a blank, at least from the bigger colleges. The Presbyterians of Hampden-Sydney defeated William & Mary to guarantee at least a share of the Virginia small-college crown for the winners, but no one bothered to record attendance. The one game Norfolk could depend on ended up at Raleigh, North Carolina, where Washington and Lee defeated North Carolina.

In 1917, despite World War I, North Carolina A&M and Virginia Tech returned to League Park to produce a low-scoring tie before a small crowd of 3,500. It was "not the greatest exhibition of the gentle pastime of football that has ever been staged on the local gridiron, nor was it the worst," wrote a reporter. The Thanksgiving contest that year pitted the Wake Forest Baptists against the Hampden-Sydney Presbyterians. It too, produced a 7-7 tie and a slim "throng of fans." Hopes of bringing the Virginia-North Carolina game to Norfolk pretty much ended in 1917 when the two schools decided to play alternately on each other's home field, even though the one in Chapel Hill only held about 3,500 fans at the time.[16]

With Norfolk totally absorbed with World War I and considerable military football in the area, collegiate contests were not played in either 1918 or 1919, except that North Carolina State sent its freshman squad to lose to the local independent Sewanees (likely named in honor of the renowned collegiate football power of the same name) in Portsmouth on Thanksgiving.

The reasons for the declining attendance at collegiate football games in the Norfolk area in the latter part of the century's second decade are hard to pinpoint. Possibly some people did not like the new game of football, preferring the rougher, grinding type of former times. It is more likely that the novelty of watching football wore off. Reporters who had previously taken great pains to build up excitement for various games now devoted less space in the days leading up to the games, and they also reduced their coverage.

Nationally, interest in collegiate football exploded in the 1920s, as colleges and some cities erected large stadiums, but the "Golden Age of College Football" had only limited impact on the Old Dominion. The heyday of Virginia collegiate football was seemingly already over by that time. Norfolk business interests avidly lobbied to make the city a center for rivalries involving various football powers, but despite their best efforts, the games that might attract big crowds usually ended up somewhere else. League Park did resume as the site of the annual VPI-Carolina State clash on Armistice Day (November 11), 1920, with 5,000 seeing the Aggies prevail. The next year a still larger crowd (8,000) saw Tech rally for a win. Being warned that poor attendance would likely end any possibility that Norfolk could expect to continue to attract the region's major colleges, business interests decorated the city for the occasion, but the intense efforts could not be sustained, and in 1923 the top attendance for a collegiate contest at League Park fell to below 4,000. In one of those contests, William & Mary had an easy time against Hampden-Sydney. The next year in early November, the morning newspaper announced that college elevens were passing up Norfolk because of the poor turnouts the previous fall. A 1925 editorial in Norfolk's morning paper expressed the belief that the bigger schools were carrying out a "football boycott" against Norfolk, the only game played over two years being between William & Mary and Trinity College (Duke University), a game incidentally won by W&M's Indians.[17]

Finally, in October 1926, 12,000 jammed into League Park to watch Tech subdue the University of Maryland, 24-8, in a contest reminiscent of some of those early in the century, as parades and serpentine dances took place before the contest, and blaring bands and heartfelt college yells accompanied it. The attendance tied the record established in 1905, but Norfolk had twice the population to draw from at the later date; however, this level of support could not be sustained. In 1927 only 3,000 came out to see the Chattanooga Moccasins defeat William & Mary, 12-7. The winners, their coach being from Notre Dame, resorted to the famed Knute Rockne offensive strategy. The next year, a more respectable number (9,000) more than filled all the seats in League Park as Tech edged the University of Maryland Terrapins, 9-6. That year, also, the powerful Quantico Marines ground down tiny Washington College, 57-0, before but 2,000 doubtless bored spectators. In 1930 Maryland and Virginia Tech played the lone major college game in Norfolk to a small crowd in Bain Field, known as League Park until rebuilt after a spectacular fire earlier that year and renamed for P. D. Bain, the late president of the American Peanut Corporation, which owned the property.[18]

Because football had originally developed in elite colleges, a certain aura surrounded collegiate games, and thus failure to attract such contests suggested some sort of stigma, but by this point the sport had become ingrained, even in the Norfolk area. Many institutions fielded teams. Starting in 1919, for example, the Newport News Shipbuilding and Drydock Company ran competitive football clubs at its Apprentice School. Although it sometimes played freshmen from the biggest colleges, it also often defeated teams from the varsities of the smaller colleges in the state.

Norfolk and other communities had well-developed football programs at their local high schools as well. Maury in Norfolk, Wilson in Portsmouth, as well as Hampton, Newport News, Suffolk and even South Norfolk possessed vibrant football programs. The same could be said for Booker T. Washington in Norfolk, Huntington in Newport News, and I. C. Norcom in Portsmouth among the black high schools. Although most of the games attracted from a few hundred to a few thousand, the annual Thanksgiving clash between Maury and Wilson drew between 6,000 and 10,000. In addition, junior varsities carried out contests, as did some junior high schools. Around this time, several junior highs participated in a soccer league in the fall, but most cities also had community recreational football leagues, the Madison Ward Community League being closest to the Division. Several men that played for the Division started out playing football within this recreational league, and for many that was the extent of their football experience when they came to college.

In the absence of regular collegiate football, participants and fans could take advantage of games put on by athletic clubs. Independent football clubs started in the area as early as 1892 when the Young Men's Christian Association club first played. Over the years, after the YMCA dropped interest in football in favor of basketball and other sports, numerous other organizations appeared on the scene. The most well known of the pre-World War I clubs, the Norfolk Light Artillery Blues, attracted a considerable following and played a varied schedule. In 1910, for example, they entertained Gallaudet College, the Washington, D.C. school for the deaf, whose best player, a Native American named Batista, matched up well against Norfolk High School graduate and VPI quarterback Billy Feurstein, who also became a famous motorcycle racer. The home club prevailed, 5-0.

In 1912, the University of Virginia beat the Blues in Charlottesville, 7-0, in what was thought to be the best-played game of the season. In 1916, the Blues carried their guns and footballs from their armory on Hampton Boulevard (the land on which it stood is now part of the ODU campus) into northern Mexico in pursuit of Pancho Villa. But they not only failed to fix their sights on the bandit, they also lost, 76-0, to Texas A&M in football.[19]

Before World War I, several military installations and ships routinely outfitted teams. The *USS Franklin* traditionally had among the best. The crew of the receiver ship often played the Blues to a standstill and even gave North Carolina A&M quite a battle down in Raleigh. The Navy Yard also sported clubs, and during World War I, the Navy Base developed a powerful squad that often defeated other East Coast bases. On Thanksgiving 1920, some 15,000 saw the Great Lakes Naval Station club best the Hampton Roads Training Station eleven at the base.[20]

For the reporters of the time, the athletic clubs yielded a great deal of interest. Reporters described hard defensive battles, some played in late December or in early January. In the early 1920s Norfolk had a city league, with teams like the Berkley Bears vying with the old Norfolk Light Artillery Blues (technically the 111th Field Artillery). The team kept the old name and sometimes had the 111th band play for them, but a direct affiliation probably no longer existed.

By the mid-1920s, the Clancy Athletic Club had joined the others, probably as an outgrowth of an old fraternity in the Norfolk neighborhood of Brambleton. There was also a Madison Athletic Club, possibly operating out of the area that had once been the Norfolk's Madison Ward (Norfolk's ward system was discontinued in 1918). These league teams played each other as well as other area clubs, such as the Sewanee Athletic Club from Portsmouth, which won the Tidewater title in 1921, or even the military clubs, some of them representing ships that happened to be in the harbor. The Richmond Athletic Club beat out the Norfolk Athletic Club for the state "colored championship" that same year.[21]

Some of the players attained celebrity status. One of the stars for Sewanee was Charles Borjes, an end who also played some minor league baseball for the local Norfolk Tars and other teams in the Virginia League. In the 1930s and for many years, Borjes, an enthusiastic advocate of sports, took pictures for *The Virginian-Pilot*. A good many of the photographs in this book are his work. Francis "Red" Barron played right end for the Clancies Athletic Club and later opened a Shell station right across Hampton Boulevard from the Norfolk Division campus. But the best-known of all was Jake Versprille, who started out with the Norfolk Navy Air Station and perhaps first gained prominence when his team shellacked the "Smoke Eaters," otherwise known as the Firemen Athletic Club, 72-12, in December 1924. After this occasion, his name appeared nearly every week for every fall over the next several years. He joined the Clancies for a season, but then switched to the Blues. In December 1926, the Blues played Harold "Red" Grange and his touring professionals, called the Americans (mostly collegiate all stars), at League Park. Even though the visitors easily won, Versprille created great excitement and local pride when he ran one play 65 yards against the greatest assemblage of football talent that local fans of that era would ever see. An account of the game written several years later claimed that it was so cold that the fans danced the Charleston to stay warm. Over the next few seasons, news accounts describe several occasions when he quarterbacked the Blues to wins and occasionally broke away for one or two of his patented long runs.[22]

Focusing on Versprille may give the wrong impression about the kind of football these men played. Broken-field scores were a relative rarity. More typical would be the games between Sewanee and one of the Norfolk teams played in late December or early January, which often as not ended as scoreless ties. Indeed, in more than one year, the two rivals played each other twice over less than a week, with neither team scoring. The weather and introduction of collegians home for the Christmas holidays and unfamiliar with the club playbook possibly held down the offenses. However, when Sewanee played a team composed of local collegiate all stars, there was a lot of scoring, most of it by the collegians.

Starting about the middle of the 1920s, the fraternal associations began to play many of their contests on Sunday afternoon. This trend may have something to do with the efforts of Frank Lawrence of Portsmouth to introduce professional baseball on the Sabbath. He failed to achieve his objective, but in the process, most sports-minded folks found out that the old Blue Laws were really not what prevented playing on Sunday. The 1877 law simply said that one could not be paid for doing on Sunday what one did the other days of the week to earn a living. Even though Norfolk's football league of the early 1920s was described as an association of amateurs, everyone knew that some players received payment, likely a share of fan donations. One Sunday game in 1927, with Versprille starring for the Blues in a win over the Doughboys (both belonged to the Norfolk, South Norfolk and Portsmouth Tri-City League at the time, which was described as semi-professional), some 6,000 came to League Park. The fans came up with but $500, which the reporter thought was a pretty paltry amount. The next year, a crowd of 8,000 donated $1,200, which seemed an acceptable level of support. The South Norfolk Panthers lost to the Doughboys in 1928, before 7,500 the day after Virginia Tech and Maryland attracted 9,000 on a Saturday. In other words, semi-pro football on Sundays was almost as popular as the top collegiate game of the year in Norfolk.[23]

In November 1900, the first major collegiate game in Norfolk took place at League Park. The contest pitted the University of Virginia against the University of North Carolina. The Virginia Cavaliers won, 17–0, in a game that supposedly determined the championship of the South before 6,000 fans. These two illustrations taken from The Virginian-Pilot *show players on the field of battle as well as gentlemen and young ladies in full fashion on the sidelines and in the stands.*

This postcard shows an October 23. 1915 game between the Norfolk Artillery Blues and USS Vermont. *The Blues would win the game 28-0. Charles Borges, long time* Virginian-Pilot *photographer, who has many photographs in his book, played for the Blues.* (From the Collection of Tom Garrett and Clay Shampoe)

This classic image is of Norfolk High School's 1905 team. (Courtesy of Sargeant Memorial Room, Norfolk Public Library)

This photograph taken at a filled Bain Field is of the November 27, 1930 Thanksgiving Day ballgame between Norfolk's Maury High School and its chief rival from Portsmouth, Woodrow Wilson High. Maury would win the game 19-0. (Courtesy of Sargeant Memorial Room, Norfolk Public Library)

CHAPTER TWO

Depression-Era Football: The Norfolk Division, 1930-1935

It was a warm, dry, mid-September day in 1930 when the Norfolk Division of the College of William & Mary opened the doors of the old Larchmont School, located on the northwest corner of Hampton Boulevard and Bolling Avenue. Before that, on September 2, a reporter asked H. Edgar Timmerman, the recently hired first director of the school whether there would be an athletic program. He said there would most likely be freshmen basketball, but "it would be impossible to follow a football schedule until later." Timmerman clearly changed his mind, because five days later, Dr. J. A .C. Chandler of the College of William & Mary hired Tom Scott to direct athletics at the new institution; the job included coaching a football team.

Scott was a multi-sport star at Maury High School: an end on the 1925 football team, a guard on the state-championship basketball club and an outfielder for the Commodores' baseball club. Known for his speed and leadership, the youthful-looking "Scotty" had just graduated from Virginia Military Institute, where he excelled in several sports, being an All-Star football selection in the Southern Conference and an honorable mention on the Associated Press All-American team. As soon as classes started, he called for candidates for the Division football team, secured permission from the city to use the field next to the new Larchmont Elementary School for practice and made arrangements with the parent school for equipment.[1]

The year before (1929), a 350-plus-page report funded by the Carnegie Foundation concluded that three-quarters of 130 colleges and universities exhibited serious ethical problems, from funds for recruitment to bogus academic credit for work not done by students or done by others for them. The only programs that seemed not so stigmatized were those that had consistently losing records or who had played less than challenging schedules. News of the ever-worsening Depression may well have detracted from publicity about the report, but it was more likely that football was too entrenched in the colleges to allow reforms even in the best of times.[2]

The new junior college on Hampton Boulevard commenced its work some 10 months after the precipitous fall of the stock market and in the midst of an economic downturn. At the same time the school opened, Governor John Pollard of Virginia, aboard a ship just off Cape Henry, Virginia, dropped a coffin labeled “Old Man Business D. Pression” into the water, but this symbolic deep-sixing of the Depression did little to stop the slide into what became the worst economic slump the nation had ever endured. The presence of the military and a broad service economy somewhat cushioned the impact of the Depression on the local area.[3]

About a week after starting practice, the Division lost its first game, 7-0, against Suffolk High School at the latter’s field. According to the press, a large crowd, including many of the college’s students, attended the game. High temperatures hurt the performance of both teams. The headline claimed “Junior College Defeats Suffolk” and “Tommy Scott’s Boys Take Measure of High Eleven, 7-0,” but a close reading of the contents reveals that Suffolk won the game. Perhaps the headline composer had a hard time accepting the fact that the older boys could lose such a contest, but with only about a week of practice, and with only a few that had actually played first string on a high school eleven, such a result could have been predicted.[4]

At the beginning of the season, the Division had a quarterback named Terry Maxey, the brother of famed Clarence “Red” Maxey, a halfback and star at the College of William & Mary. But Terry had apparently never played high school football. Halfback Jack

Hawkins had experience and potential, having played at Blackstone Military Academy (Virginia) and for the University of North Carolina freshmen. He was also the brother of Al Hawkins, captain at VMI the previous year. Frank "Junie" Wilson, soon to be appointed captain of the club, had played at Maury in 1928.

A week after the Suffolk loss, at Bain Field, "Tommy Scott's Warriors" hammered Oceana High School, the secondary school located near the resort city of Virginia Beach. "Greatly improved over their previous performance," and showing "promise of developing into a dangerous gridiron squad," the Division club, "composed mostly of local lads" romped, 47-0, before a small but enthusiastic crowd. Hawkins, Wilson, and Billy Walker led the potent offense against Oceana, the last-mentioned receiving special note for his ability to circle ends for long gains. Billy, as a student at Christ Church School, had set state records in the 100-yard dash. A noteworthy aspect of this contest is that it was played under floodlights and was the second night football contest ever played in Norfolk and the first Friday night encounter. The first contest under the lights, played the Saturday before, pitted the Sewanee club out of Portsmouth and the South Norfolk Panthers.[5]

The ensuing Friday evening, the Norfolk Division, now known as the Braves (the afternoon newspaper reporter called them the "Willies," presumably for the William part of the school name), tamed the Tigers of South Norfolk High School, 6-0. The game remained tied until Terry Maxey intercepted the "oval from the ozone, shook off a couple of opponents and dashed like a scared rabbit" for the only score. Given that South Norfolk was about on a par with Suffolk, the win demonstrated that Scott's men were getting better, and the reporter expected when they learned the "finer points of the game," the "comparatively lightweight team" would "make up in speed" what "they lack in beef."[6]

The next Wednesday, nearly the "entire student body" of the Division boarded special busses, crossed Hampton Roads on the ferry, and made its way to Williamsburg, where that afternoon the team took on the College of William & Mary "Indian Freshmen" in the biggest game of the year for the new college. The home team took an early 7-0 lead, but in the third quarter Jack Hawkins drove across the rival goal after Bill Abrams went off-tackle for 30 yards. But the attempt for the extra point failed. With about two minutes remaining, halfback Billy Walker took a long pass from quarterback Maxey and outran the defense for another 30 yards for a touchdown. Another account credits Sam Phillips with a 30-yard run around end to set up the final score and the 13-7 Norfolk Division win. That evening, the students celebrated their win with a pageant at the school. The newspaper at the Williamsburg campus did not give an account of the game, but it later disclosed that the Division had actually played the frosh "B" team.[7]

In another Friday night game under the lights at Bain Field, the Division pummeled Hertford High School (Perquimans County High School by one account), North Carolina, 24-7, in a game in which the Braves used their second string for much of the game. That gave Bill Eames, the substitute right tackle, a chance to score on a 75-yard interception.[8]

On the last afternoon of October, the Division once again faced the freshmen from the College of William & Mary. The losers of the first encounter thought that overconfidence and luck had led to their previous downfall, so the "Papooses" challenged the Braves. Scott insisted that the game be played in Norfolk. Even though a muddy—almost treacherous—field slowed down the speedy Braves, they still amassed 12 first downs to 3 for the visitors. Walker even got off one of his patented 30-yard dashes. Although Norfolk dominated the game, they could only attain a scoreless tie against their rivals. The parent institution's newspaper heading said "Frosh Scrubs Battle to Tie," with "Tommy Scott's minions." That game ended the brief season for the Braves with a record of 4 wins and 1 loss against "B" level high schools and the William & Mary freshman "B" team.[9]

In the fall of 1930, Atlantic University, a private college inspired by the mystic Edgar Cayce and backed by New York financiers, commenced its brief career on the shores of Virginia Beach. Further along in preparing for its fall opening than the Division, the resort college hired a coach several months earlier than the Division, giving more time to recruit players, arrange a more complete schedule, and create a field near Virginia Beach's new Cavalier Hotel. Atlantic University, known as the Sea Dogs (legend says they had a three-legged dog as a mascot), played a full slate, winning over Baltimore University, Lynchburg College, Newport News Apprentice and American University, and losing to Appalachian State Teachers College, Atlantic Christian College and the Quantico Marines. The only lopsided loss was to the latter, a powerful military team, at Bain in a night game before about 1,600.

As the regular football season neared its end, the headmaster of Norfolk Academy, Edward N. Smith, strongly urged the Division to take on Atlantic University at Bain Field, with the receipts from the contest helping the increasing numbers of unemployed residents. But nothing came from this suggestion at that time, possibly because the Division team had disbanded for the year or because Scott realized the Sea Dogs had played a much more challenging schedule. In December, Director Timmerman announced that he had arranged for grading and grassing the field south of Bolling Avenue (the current site of structures honoring William Spong, Alfred Rollins, and James Koch). Timmerman hoped everything would be ready for baseball in the spring and football the next fall.[10]

In January, the school honored the hard work the young men put in on behalf of the Division by organizing a Monogram Club, composed only of those who had received their letters. Timmerman talked about the difficulty of having any season at all in 1930 and praised Coach Scott and the team for loyalty and hard work under difficult circumstances. Timmerman also lauded the local newspapers for their coverage of the season. Headmaster Smith of Norfolk Academy asked the audience to remember the scrubs, whose names never reached the public eye, letters went to 21 participants. All the lettermen received green sweaters, even though the football uniforms did not take that color until the mid-1930s, after which on rare occasions reporters referred to the Division as the "Green Wave."[11]

Because Scott had more time to work on a schedule and would have greater player experience and preparation, folks figured on a better result in the fall of 1931. Perhaps because it was becoming increasingly difficult to find jobs, there were more than twice the number of students now attending classes at the renamed Norfolk Division of the College of William & Mary and Virginia Polytechnic Institute. About 50 of them tried out for the football squad, so Scott had about twice the number to pick a team from as he had the first year. That number was roughly 20 percent of the males attending the college, with women comprising about 40 percent of the student body, unlike in high schools, where girls outnumbered boys. Turnout rates for football were traditionally high at local high schools, with Maury, with a large student base, often having 150 students on the practice field on the first day. Coach Dick Fletcher sometimes cut as many as 50 players at a time to pare down the number to an acceptable level. It is quite likely that many of those who played for the Division were among those cut from Maury squads over the years.

the Division tuned up for the season against the Presidents of Woodrow Wilson High School at the old Washington Street Park in Portsmouth. With both schools using as many players as possible, the "Baby Indians" rolled up a 32-6 advantage. Billy Morgan, a former star at South Norfolk High School, did well at quarterback in guiding several successful drives. The following week, Scott took 26 men over to South Norfolk, where the Tigers were no match, as 1,500 fans watched the "speedy backfield combination" and a strong defense romp to a 39-0 win. Fullback Ernie Wooten repeatedly battered the high school line.[12]

But the season lost some of its glitter when the Braves faced the freshmen from Catholic University, a leading football power. Averaging 20 pounds less per man, the defense held its own until the last quarter, when the visitors broke through for two scores, the first coming indirectly as a result of an interception. During the struggle, as might be expected in this situation, several Norfolk men sustained injuries. Among the injured were Wooten and Hawkins as well as Morgan, and in the ensuing practices Terry Maxey, now recovered from an ankle injury, took over at quarterback again and Bill Abrams, who had played for Maury two years before, became one of the halfbacks. Herman "Rummy" Robinette, another one-time Maury man, took over at fullback.[13]

Just before the loss to Catholic, the editor of the student newspaper took up the question of whether football was "harmful or helpful." The sport ruled most campuses in the fall, he observed, disturbing professors who contended with declining attendance on Saturday afternoons (in those rare schools where classes were still taught on Saturdays). On the positive side, playing football channeled emotions and increased student spirit. Anything worthwhile in life took time and effort, and football was a "deep and influencing part of college life." Moreover, modern players had to be of high intelligence, because the sport focused less on beef and more on speed and deception. Even adults picked up the excitement, paid to see the games, and "carried the spirit in their souls." Despite the editor's decision that football was not harmful, the issue would remain unresolved in academia.[14]

But by the time of the next game, against Maury High School, Wooten and Hawkins had returned. The added depth, along with several new plays, made the Braves the favorite. As described in an article written in the morning daily by the venerable Sam Potts, the Division's aerial attack before some 2,000 at Bain Field easily overcame the younger Commodores, 34-6. Robinette, at halfback, made a spectacular 55-yard punt return.[15]

In a hard-fought struggle against the Elizabeth City High School Jackets, the Braves scored two touchdowns in the second half on the road to win, 13-12. Usually one would make little of defeating a high school, but in this case, the North Carolina school had not been defeated by anyone for two years and ranked as the Tar Heel State champions in the category in which they competed. Its line averaged 185 pounds, 20 pounds more than the visitors' average player. One of the literary contributors to the campus paper joked about the trip into the "the wilderness, known to the civilized world as North Carolina" and seeing Elizabeth City in "its Oriental splendor." After the sarcastic reference to the city on the Pasquotank River, the Division student claimed he and his friends paid differing amounts for tickets to the game (some paying 25 cents and others twice that amount), with girls admitted for free. The seats proved less than desirable (he sat on a protruding nail in the stands). Becoming so enamored with his effort to provide "local color," the writer failed to provide an account of the game.[16]

the Division then took on the freshmen from the College of William & Mary at Williamsburg, considered to be the best freshman squad in the state at the time, and probably on a par with the team from Catholic. Predictably, Scott's men succumbed, 12-0, with both scores coming early in the contest, one resulting from an interception on the Norfolk 20 and a subsequent plunge over tackle, and the second from a sustained drive coming on the heels of the first score. The battered visitors then settled down, but their sputtering offense and tougher defense produced a series of punts for both sides, creating something of a boring contest, made more tedious by the frequent delays caused by injuries to Norfolk players. The Williamsburg campus paper credited the Extension eleven with being "plucky."[17]

In early October, the number of players had fallen to 21, at which time the college newspaper provided data on the team. The players ranged in weight from 123 to 180 pounds with an average of about 156. They varied in height between 5 feet 5 inches and 6 feet 1 inch. Fullback Wooten, who could also punt, weighed the most and stood at 5 feet 8 inches, while quarterback Morgan was the shortest and weighed but 141 pounds. These weights compared favorably to those of high school athletes and even some of the freshmen teams the Division would play, but fell considerably shy of some of the junior colleges or colleges the Braves would come up against. The club seemed to embody the traits of its coach. Like Tommy Scott, they were small, but fast and scrappy.[18]

A two-week gap in the schedule gave the Norfolk lads time to recuperate from the recent battles, but this lapse did not please the editor of the campus newspaper. The editor doubted that other schools backed out of games, or that injuries caused cancellations. More games should have been arranged for the current season. He pointed out that students paid a $7.50 athletic fee each semester, part of which provided a free pass to athletic events. The athletic fee seemed high when compared to the $37.50 per semester to cover a full slate of courses. He complained about there being but two home games thus far in the season, an insufficient number given the fees paid. Even if the games against Wingate Junior College and Campbell College (both in North Carolina) came through, which seemed questionable, the college still trailed Maury in the number of home contests. The editor said nothing about the fact that thus far in the season, the Division had only beaten high schools and had lost both encounters with freshmen teams.[19]

Whatever the basis for the criticism, a shift in momentum took place. Wingate Junior College, which had defeated many North Carolina two-year colleges and tied Newport News Apprentice, came to town. Their tackles weighed well over 200 pounds apiece, with the average lineman coming in at 180, the weight of Norfolk's biggest player. Moreover, with the loss of Jack Hawkins, Sam Phillips, "Pop" Bowen, and Jeter Kaufman due to the lack of "scholastic yardage" and Robinette's cracked rib, the Division varsity seemed especially vulnerable. But Morgan returned, now converted to halfback with little Maxey directing the plays. On Armistice Day that year, substitute Earl "Pepper and Salt" Martin (possibly the first part of the nickname was in honor of the St. Louis Cardinal hero in the World Series that year) dazzled everyone at Bain, when in the second quarter, he belatedly covered a ball that had been punted from Wingate's 20-yard line, which bounced along to the Division's 10. Realizing that the ball would probably stop well within his 10-yard marker, Earl grabbed the oval, and after faking to the right, he reversed field and with the help of a Maxey block and interference by other mates, he stiff-armed and weaved his way for some 99 yards. Morgan flipped a pass to Maxey for the extra point, and a 7-0 lead. That run gave the Norfolk players enough courage to hold off the heavier Wingate players, a verdict secured when Morgan intercepted a pass late in the contest.[20]

With renewed hope, Scott's men prepared for Campbell College from North Carolina at Bain Field. Again, with eligibility rules resurfacing and with Captain Junie Wilson ill, it looked like a forthcoming uphill struggle in the final home game of the season. On the day of the game, however, Norfolk proved to have the dominant and more experienced team, but although they secured more first downs—11-8—the game ended scoreless. Earl Martin nearly duplicated his earlier famous run when he picked up a fumble behind his own goal line and rambled to the 50-yard line, where a lone safety finally brought him down.[21]

Another editorial in the campus paper urged everyone to attend an impromptu game against Atlantic University. Although not on the original schedule, school management must have taken the criticism about the lack of home contests to heart. Almost a year after Norfolk Academy's headmaster had suggested a game between the two local colleges, the teams finally played each other. As originally suggested, gate receipts would be aimed for the newly unemployed and added to the budget of the Community Fund, which had already raised about $280,000. Because fans "liked nothing better than a well-played football game" between two "well-matched teams," especially for charity, he assumed the crowd would fill Bain Field.[22]

Although the attendance fell far short of what was expected or needed, the 2,000 that attended the game added $1,200 for relief for the city's poor. Astoundingly, the Division had a comparatively easy time overcoming the resort city's representative, even though the latter had heavier players. At least one of the previous year's Atlantic players (Sid Sachs, who also played basketball) and the line coach had switched to Norfolk, when Atlantic hired a new head coach, suggesting that finances were increasingly hampering the new private university. Their record in defeating the crew of one of the local Navy ships, tying the Sewanee Athletic Club at Portsmouth, losing narrowly to Catawba (North Carolina) and being mopped up by Langley Air Force Base and Shenandoah College (Virginia) was less impressive than the results of the year before, but they still looked like they had enough to beat the Braves. During the game, the Seadogs had one more first down than Norfolk and gained much terrain between the 30-yard lines in the second half, but they failed to score. Norfolk scored early after being backed up on its own 2-yard marker. Maxey capped a sustained drive, sneaking over the goal, being so small he seemed lost in the pile of players. The quarterback passed for the extra point (Norfolk lacked a drop kicker). In the fourth quarter, a series of Maxey passes against a "leaking" Atlantic defense brought another touchdown, the last on a pass to Earl Martin, winning, 19-0.

After the season, Atlantic University, absent the $5,000 a month subsidy from New

York financiers, went into receivership and later closed its doors, another victim of the Great Depression. What could have been a great football rivalry died a glimmering. The Division received the defunct school's books, some of its lab equipment and athletes like big Mike Cavish.[23]

The Atlantic game brought the season to a close, Norfolk having outscored its opponents 127-31, with 6 wins, 2 losses, and 1 tie. The Division had originally planned to go to Florida to play the University of Miami on December 18, but for unexplained reasons the contest did not take place until October of the next year. Atlantic University was supposed to play Miami the day after Christmas in the Sunshine State in 1931, but the financial problems of the school obviously made that impossible. The performance of the Division under Scott, with a much more demanding schedule than played the previous year must have heartened fans, but because the institution had completed two years, some of its players would be leaving. Also, many players decided not to return for various reasons. The high turnover made it hard to produce a consistently competitive eleven, at least compared to the teams Norfolk played.

The middle of September 1932, came in with little improvement in the economy and only about 300 showing up to take classes at the Norfolk Division, but with 22 of them reporting to Scott. A few others showed up later in the month. Late the previous year, Scott had arranged for a 10-game schedule, subject to change. The Oak Ridge Prep game disappeared, seemingly replaced by one with Miami University. Scott welcomed back Terry Maxey, Tommy Nee, William Abrams and several other veterans. Jack Hawkins remained undecided about his status. The former Atlantic University player Mike Cavish, at 190 pounds, looked like a potential fullback. Jack Darden, a one-time star for William & Mary, was helping to get the men in shape, but he really wanted to return to Williamsburg and play for the big Braves.[24]

The Braves had little trouble disposing of South Norfolk High School before 1,200 at Bain, winning 18-0 with 14 first downs to but one for South Norfolk's Tigers. Jack Hawkins displayed some talent in punting the ball. Woodrow Wilson did even worse, being shut out at the Washington Street Park, as the heavier and more experienced Braves wore them down under the early fall sun in what probably should be considered an exhibition. During the early part of the season, the Braves also scrimmaged with Maury, the Division's second team giving way to Maury but its first string opening up huge holes for Wilson and Cavish to break away on long gains.[25]

That year the Division's "Baby Indians" dominated the William & Mary freshmen, 13-0, producing 11 first downs to four for the visitors. Mike Cavish, the big left-handed halfback, surprised everyone when he threw the ball. Jack Saunders, the left tackle, starred on defense, once breaking through to block a punt in back of the William & Mary goal, which allowed an alert Clinton Walker to score a touchdown. Right end Tom Kelly also recovered a fumble, thus ending a freshmen threat. Only some long punts by the William & Mary quarterback kept the score down. One account attributed the comparatively easy win to the weight and experience of the Division eleven.[26]

Twenty-five of Scott's men then took a bus to North Carolina, where they were shut out by the freshmen from Wake Forest, 6-0. In that contest, Norfolk's aerial attack produced 11 first downs compared to eight for the home team. The Wake Forest press particularly praised Jack Hawkins's long passes in the first quarter and mentioned Terry Maxey as another standout.[27]

In mid-October, the team faced its biggest challenge, not only for the season, but probably for the entire existence of the football program. The previous season's anticipated late-season game against Miami University was rescheduled when a potential Hurricane adversary backed out of its commitment. W. N. "Bill" Cox, the sports columnist, who had fairly recently started writing for Norfolk's morning paper, thought Scott's decision to play such a prestigious school "must be the exuberance of youth, the fitness of good health and other traits that go with being young and strong." While a more experienced coach might have balked at the idea, Scott readily accepted the invitation to journey with his youngsters to Florida by special train. Arriving in time to practice Thursday night, the team stayed at the Ponce de Leon Hotel. Friday night they took on Miami before 10,000 fans at the site of what later became the Orange Bowl. "Norfolk Division Eleven Goes down Fighting, 6-0," the headline incorrectly read (the actual score being 6-2), as Norfolk reached its rival's 20-yard line late in the game, after benefitting from several passes from Junie Wilson to Terry Maxey. At that point an interception saved Miami from a possible embarrassing loss to Norfolk's junior college.[28]

For years afterward, folks talked about this highlight game, saying that Miami had not really intended to invite a junior college to play, but wanted William & Mary to send a team. It is possible that the invitation ended up in Norfolk in error and thus initiated conversations about a game between the two schools in 1931. But by the fall of the next year, folks in Miami not only knew the proper name of the opposition, they even had foreknowledge of the style the Division played, it being adapted from Pop Warner's tactics. Warner developed his wing formation early in the century largely to increase passing potential, believing that the T-formation, then in use, only permitted a sound running game. When the rules changed to permit forward passing, several coaches, including Warner as well as Fielding Yost, Amos Alonzo Stagg and John Heisman, gave up on the older system. When the T-formation returned around the time of World War II, Warner expressed the view that it would soon be replaced with more pass-oriented offenses, where someone other than the quarterback would likely put the ball in the air.[29]

Rhea Walker, who played for the Division's 1932 team but did not participate in the Miami game, explained that the team operated out of a single or sometimes a double wing, with the center snapping the ball directly to one of four pre-selected backs.[30]

Tommy McCann, "the Waukegan Wizard," who had started coaching at Miami the previous year, had his freshmen use Warner-style plays against his first string. McCann had shifted his type of offense from the Knute Rockne-Notre Dame-style to that of Bob Zuppke, at the University of Illinois, where the great Red Grange had played. Whether Tom Scott had this piece of information is not known.

Pregame news coverage in Miami about the game not only discussed the style of offenses to be deployed, but also revealed that the home team did not enjoy an advantage in average weight, a fact that surprised the Miami press and led them to think that the game might be closer than experts had figured. The account of the game at Moore's Field in Miami in the Florida newspaper opens with, "Well! William & Mary, Norfolk branch or any other branch seems to know things about this game of football. And the University of Miami Hurricanes, playing their first game against a visiting team that has been to the post three times already this fall, was forced to battle every minute to turn back a determined band of invaders, 6-2." Fans came to the game expecting weak adversaries, but were satisfied when their eleven rose to the occasion. Although the 'Canes dominated the first quarter, scoring a touchdown and nearly making another, the young visitors "fought like tigers." Fans saw "some corking good football," and also a stupid move on the part of one of the Miami backs, who lost 21 yards by running the wrong way, taking his team out of field-goal range. A sophomore quarterback led the winning play, scoring by going through a hole left of tackle. The extra-point attempt failed when the kicker moved too slowly and "an alert visitor" broke though a hole to block the kick. The second half proved to be a struggle, with penalties on both elevens, partially due to indecisive officials. Norfolk scored its two points late in the game when Hawkins launched a 52-yard punt into a corner, and the Miami back retreated behind his own goal to escape being tackled and ended up yielding a safety. When Junie Wilson started to connect on his passes, Miami devised better pass coverage, leading to several interceptions. When Wilson broke his hand, Jack Hawkins tried his hand at passing, but Miami intercepted the ball one more time, thus ending Norfolk's final threat.[31]

The legend of the Miami game grew over the years, partially because the Florida school came to be a great football power. In 1931 and 1932, the Hurricanes were a pretty low-level storm. The previous year they had lost to Western Kentucky by a wide margin and barely managed to beat Rollins College in winning four and losing eight. The more experienced 1932 version did better, winning four and losing three. Still, that a junior college almost beat a full-fledged college is rather surprising.

In the wake of their loss to Miami, the Braves traveled to Dayton, Virginia to take on the Shenandoah College eleven on a Friday afternoon in late October. In a comparatively high-scoring affair, the Division allowed the home team to grab a lead, mostly on a 50-yard punt return, but on the ensuing kickoff, the Braves tied the score, when Mike Cavish plunged over the goal line, with Maxey passing to Bill Thomas for the extra point, putting Norfolk ahead. The second half featured two more Norfolk touchdowns, one resulting indirectly from a Cavish interception, followed by a Maxey carry for another six points. Jake Saunders and Bill Thomas performed admirably in the 26-12 win. Rhea Walker credits Shenandoah with having more flat rocks on its playing field than any other school. He remembers that fact well because his head struck one of them, knocking him out.[32]

The next week, the Braves returned home, where they dominated North Carolina's Louisburg College. Maxey and Cavish each scored two touchdowns, three the results of sustained drives. Maxey's 70-yard ramble through the opposition on a punt return produced the fourth touchdown. A safety and three extra points explain the final score of 29-0.[33]

The Braves then faced the Virginia Tech freshman club that included among others, Jack Carpenter, the son of Hunter Carpenter, the greatest offensive player in Virginia during the era of old-style football, but the Carpenter name did not appear in the lineup or game account. The Tech freshmen also had "Rummy" Robinette, who played for Norfolk the previous year. Scott's men were still recovering from injuries sustained in recent games. Junie Wilson protected his fractured right hand with a special bandage. Despite these disadvantages, the Braves shut out the Little Gobblers, 13-0, before 2,500 at Bain Field in a "Spectacular Game," according to the secondary newspaper headline. Jack "Ripper" Hawkins had an outstanding game, but he also had a little luck when his low punt near the end of the first half skimmed off a rival player's helmet and bounced off a VPI player on the 21-yard line, where end Bill Thomas picked it up and galloped for a long gain. Thomas also made two critical interceptions.[34]

The next week, the Division played somewhat listlessly in the mud in a scoreless tie with the Davidson (North Carolina) frosh before fewer than 1,000 fans. The ejection of quarterback Hawkins for unnecessary roughness in the third quarter did not help the offense, but before Jack's departure, he launched a punt for 70 yards and also led the Braves in gaining ground. Thus the Division ended the home part of its schedule, its home goal line never crossed that season. In something of an anticlimax, the lads succumbed to Campbell College in North Carolina, 7-0, each club having six first downs. According to Rhea Walker, with the ball at about midfield and Norfolk in possession, the referee informed the players that more than five minutes were left in the game. On the very next play Norfolk drove to the 2-yard line, when the same official said time had expired. Despite this loss, the 1932 eleven had won six, absorbed two defeats, and had one tie.[35]

After the season, an editorial in the campus paper complained about dropping freshman teams from Wake Forest, Davidson and VPI, but praised not trying to play anyone like Miami because of the expense involved. The three frosh clubs required too high a guarantee and playing Miami was "clearly unpractical." A subsequent more detailed editorial, probably by Henry Roberts, again complained about the athletic department giving out far higher guarantees than it received to play football. The Miami game stuck out "like a sore thumb in the athletic muddle of this institution." Supposedly, 10,000 cash-paying fans saw the game, but Norfolk ended up losing the game and $400.90, as the Miami guarantee even fell short of the railroad fare. What was even more upsetting to the editor was that several members of the team convinced Scott not to schedule any more games against the freshman team from one of the North Carolina colleges. The editor's main point was the same one made before, that the $7.50 per semester athletic fee made up about 10 percent of the student expenses at the college. In three years, students had contributed $15,000, and the editor wondered what might have been accomplished if the money had been spent in ways other than paying athletic staff and covering costly trips. The editor thought it wrong to use the athletic fee to help pay coaches who should have received money for teaching required physical education courses.[36]

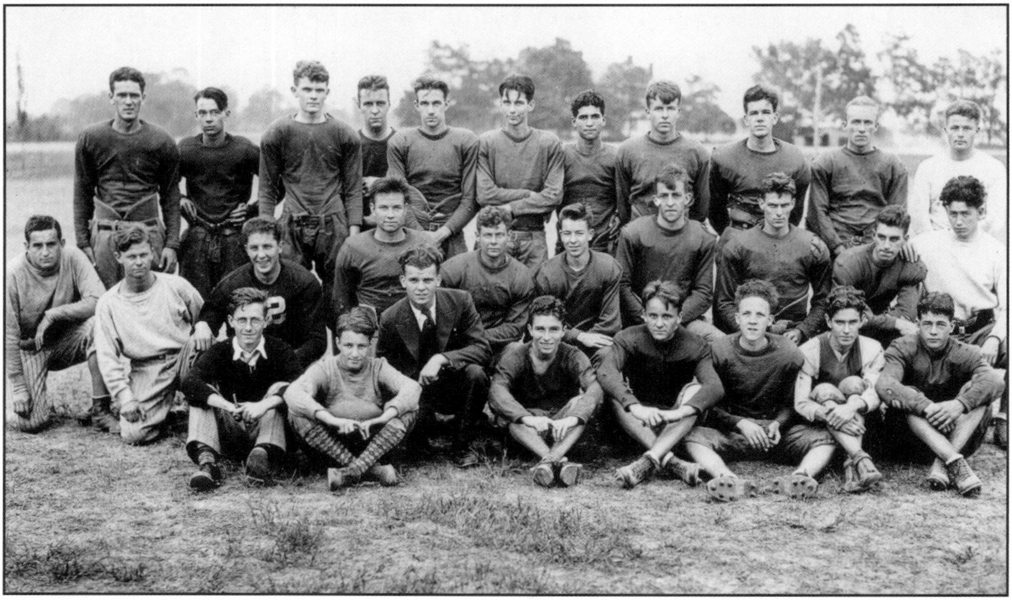

This is the only image of the 1930 Norfolk Division Braves squad in the university's archives. Unfortunately, no team members were identified except for Coach Tommy Scott (top row far right). The Braves would finish the brief season with a 4–1 record. The team was comprised of local players, many whom had never played for their respective high schools. The squad was led that season by quarterback Terry Maxey and halfbacks Frank "Junie" Wilson, Jack Hawkins, Billy Walker and Bill Abrams. (Courtesy of Special Collections and University Archives, Perry Library, Old Dominion University)

Thomas "Tommy" Scott served as the Division's first athletic director. In addition to this position, Tommy coached football, basketball, baseball and track, and taught algebra and trigonometry. A Norfolk native, this gifted athlete starred at both Maury High and Virginia Military Institute. While at VMI he became a football honorable mention All-American at left end. He also lettered in baseball and basketball for this Southern Conference school. From 1930 to 1941, Scott's influence and calm demeanor had an impact on every student he encountered. (Courtesy of Sargeant Memorial Room, Norfolk Public Library)

Harry S. Ball, who played end for the Division from 1931 to 1933, is standing in front of the new Larchmont Elementary School. A graduate of Maury High, he would play an integral part of the team for three years. Ball later became a longtime funeral director in the city. (Courtesy of Sargeant Memorial Room, Norfolk Public Library)

This photo of Bill Smart was taken on the football field located on the corner south of Bolling Avenue and Hampton Boulevard. Smart would play center for Scott's 1932 and 1933 squads. (Courtesy of Sargeant Memorial Room, Norfolk Public Library)

From 1931 to 1933, no one def ned the guard position as did Clinton Walker. Nicknamed "Jack Okie," this Maury High graduate came to the Braves after playing one year for the William & Mary freshman squad. In 1933, his leadership qualities for the Braves would be rewarded with him being appointed team captain. After anchoring the left guard position for three years, Walker returned to serve as line coach for Tommy Scott in 1934. (Courtesy of Sargeant Memorial Room, Norfolk Public Library)

Circa 1930, this area would later become the centerpiece of the young campus. The original academic building (former Larchmont Elementary) is top center and the new Larchmont Elementary is top right. The football field is across from Larchmont Elementary. (Courtesy of Sargeant Memorial Room, Norfolk Public Library)

From 1930 until 1935, Norfolk's Bain Field was the scene of most of the Norfolk Division's home games. This photograph shows a Braves game at Bain before mostly empty stands. (Courtesy of Sargeant Memorial Room, Norfolk Public Library)

CHAPTER THREE

Sustaining the Program, 1933–1935

Over the ensuing year, the American economy nearly collapsed before newly elected president Franklin Roosevelt could launch his New Deal. Roosevelt quickly stanched a bleeding banking system, as Congress substantially expanded the role of the federal government. Money raised for Norfolk's Community Fund fell by over half the 1931 amount, and the number of unemployed kept rising. By the time the next football season started, long lines waited to find jobs under the Civil Works Administration. Although critics complained about too many being hired to rake leaves, other projects included installing athletic facilities at Norfolk's Lafayette Park on Granby Street, which Maury High also used for practice, sometimes scrimmaging with the Division there. Government leaders hoped these makeshift projects might help offset the closing of the Ford Plant for retooling.

The federal government, having started numerous public works projects during Hoover's administration, had contractors finishing a new U.S. Marine Hospital near the southern end of the old Hampton Boulevard Bridge and the new post office (now known as the Federal Building) in downtown Norfolk on Granby Street. The Civilian Conservation Corps, created under Roosevelt, was signing up hundreds of young, unattached men who would, among other tasks, build facilities near Cape Henry for what would become Seashore State Park. They were paid $30 a month, $25 of which went to parents to supplement family incomes. Over the next several years, thousands of college-age men worked for the corps under military officers. The full impact of all these programs on the Norfolk Division will never be known, but the football program and the college may have lost potential students and players who opted to help out their families rather than attend college, inexpensive though such an education was. The number of those attending the Norfolk Division dropped off in 1933, so fewer candidates reported for football.

Just to enliven the situation, a hurricane blew into Norfolk in August of 1933. The rushing tide flooded a good bit of the downtown and also crashed into Willoughby Spit, even causing deaths.

The 1933 season brought back only five lettermen from the 1932 squad plus two that played in 1931 out of the 40 who had tried out for the team. The new squad would lack the experience and weight of the 1932 edition. Jack Hawkins, Mike Cavish, Junie Wilson, and Mickey Ottley were all now playing for the Norfolk Clancies. Junie later went to the Berkley Bears, another semi-pro club. Another Clancy was Buck Miles, who once played tackle for VMI and Tech, being an All-Southern selectee for the latter. When assistant coach Jack Warden returned to Williamsburg to play for the parent college, Miles became the Norfolk Division's line coach. The holdovers included Bill Smart at center, Johnny Singleton at left end, Captain Clinton Walker at guard, end Harry Ball and reserve end Bill Anderson, halfback Joe Redford, halfback Rhea Walker, and lineman Clarence "Sugar" Forehand, who had played in 1931.

Although Scott had to work with several boys whose only experience consisted of playing in the Madison Ward Community League, the club had potential among the new players. It had "flashy" quarterback Elmo Barnes, out of Emporia, Virginia. Heyward "Ace" Mercer, a 1931 graduate of Maury at 164 pounds, looked good at end; former guard Bob Richardson weighed in at 180, and Dick Dozier's 169 pounds made him the heaviest of the original backs. They looked like comers in the backfield. Dozier, a gifted natural athlete, had starred for Maury in basketball and baseball, but he never played football for the Commodores, although he did act as manager. Charlie Spence (at 166 pounds) could be a strong tackler, and Courtney Bell, a Maury halfback, had some speed as a track man. Halfback Clarence Keagey came in at 129 pounds. William Redwood had attended Woodberry Forrest. Morris Kruger (222 pounds), along with Roger Denny (216 pounds), out of

Kempsville, certainly gave some size in the line, but a reporter's assessment of the team in early October focused on the lack of weight for the club as a whole.[1]

The Braves had a successful scrimmage with Wilson High School at the latter's field, and then downed the freshmen from William & Mary at Williamsburg, 7-0, when, after Bill Smart intercepted a pass, Johnny Singleton caught the game-winning pass from Elmo Barnes. The Division got the extra point because of an offside. William & Mary's paper described the contest as hard-fought, with Norfolk stopping the Papoose passing game deep in its own territory and relying heavily on the punting of Barnes, who "played a stellar game."[2]

In the first home game of the season, the Braves took on a tough Shenandoah College eleven at Bain Field. The Hornets scored a first-quarter touchdown on a drive from about midfield, mostly on the ground. That 6-0 score stood up against various Braves attacks, including a long runback by Walker. On another occasion, Johnny Singleton caught a pass and the Braves reached inside their rival's 30. But each of the drives stalled. Later, Bob Richardson grabbed a Hornet fumble in the air and raced 36 yards, only to fumble the ball himself and turn it back over to the enemy. The closest the home team came to scoring occurred when Sugar Forehand and substitute Morris Krueger blocked a punt. A Hornet back, however, fell on the oval on his 3-yard line. And so the Braves lost another game by failing to cash in on their opportunities.[3]

Even though the players bore a lot of bruises from this encounter, they prepared hard to face their next hurdle—the even tougher freshmen from Catholic University, which the Braves played in Washington, D.C. The Division stood little chance and absorbed a 26-0 drubbing from the gigantic "Little Cardinals." Rhea Walker said that after the game Scott told his players that many of the freshmen that played against the Braves that day would play for Catholic in its next varsity game. Catholic also employed the Rockne shift, a device tending to create offside calls against defenders.[4]

At this point, Scott virtually started the season afresh by playing high schools—Maury and South Norfolk. The previous year, Maury and the Division had not played each other because the contests in 1931 had become too contentious. A reporter for *The Ledger-Dispatch* explained that before the advent of the Division, Commodore football held sway over Norfolk, and the coming of the Braves created envy among the high school lads. With the numerous close relationships of players on each team, including the friendship of coaches Tom Scott and Maury's Dick Fletcher, the contest developed an unanticipated intensity akin to a civil war.[5]

Rhea Walker contrasted the two men's coaching styles: Scott always acted calmly in pointing out problems, while Fletcher ranted a great deal at individual players. Rhea says he could never have played for Fletcher but he never had any trouble with Scott.[6]

Despite a sputtering offense, the grey-shirted Braves bested the orange-clad Maury Commodores, 6-0, before some 2,500 spectators at Bain Field. Facing fourth down with 5 yards to go in Maury territory, Barnes backed up and fired a pass to Harry Ball, who caught it at the 1-yard line amid several Maury men. Johnny Singleton, having been shifted from end to back, then plunged through for the game's only score. Another line plunge failed to bring in the extra point, but the Braves had broken through when they needed to, and as one might expect, they were "jubilant." The Braves followed up this victory by taming the South Norfolk High School Tigers, 21-6, with Singleton scoring two touchdowns and a successful extra point kick, and the second string playing for most of the second half.[7]

With the wins against the high schools and with hopes about salvaging the season revived, the Braves took on Augusta Military Academy, one of the stronger prep schools in Virginia (5-1 at the time), on a Friday afternoon, the day before Armistice Day. The Shenandoah Valley school's coach was Leigh Williams, who before starring at Washington and Lee had played with Scott on a Maury state championship basketball team. Augusta also had at least two Maury men on its roster. In the opening minutes of the contest Courtney Bell intercepted a pass on his own 10-yard line and rambled over the far end zone to give Norfolk its only touchdown of the game, followed by a Singleton successful extra point. Otherwise, the defense of the school from Fort Defiance dominated the battlefield. The Norfolk defense, however, also proved equal to the task, preserving a 7-0 victory. Only 500 fans watched the game. Possibly more would have come had it been played at night, but the lighting of Bain Field had only been temporary.[8]

In the middle of November, Scott treated the lads to a trip to the Eastern Shore to play the Cape Charles Boys' Club. The ferry ride proved enjoyable as did the game, during which Scott gave his second string lots of time, as the team rolled to a 27-0 win, with

Singleton Garrett, back-up quarterback, directing most of the offense.[9]

In a way, the success of the season now came down to the final game—to be played at Bain Field against Louisburg College. The Braves had easily overcome the Old Trap, North Carolina outfit the previous year, but the press warned that the current Louisburg edition had only narrowly lost to the William & Mary freshmen early in the season and more recently had lost to the UNC freshmen in only the last few minutes. UNC had mauled its University Virginia counterpart, 35-0. Despite the warning, Captain Elbert Burgess of the visitors scored all three touchdowns of the game, the result of a solid running attack, before the smallest crowd of the season.[10]

Just after the 1933 season, *The High Hat* again criticized the $15 annual athletic fee, only $1 of which supported the campus newspaper. But the fee covered half of Scott's salary and a portion of that of the woman who conducted physical education courses at the institution. The editor thought both were well worth their salaries, but claimed that such instructors were paid full salaries at the Williamsburg campus. The editor likely did not know that Scott's regular pay of $900 along with his $900 from the activity funds had both been cut 25 percent in 1933 due to an automatic reduction for most William & Mary faculty. Base salaries remained the same for several more years, subject only to 10 percent cuts.[11]

The 1933 season ended with a record of five wins and three losses. Although the team had defeated several high schools, the freshmen from William & Mary and Augusta Military Academy, it had lost badly to the Catholic University freshmen, and had lost its two collegiate contests of the year. But with only Harry Ball and Clinton Walker known to be finishing their careers at Division, the coaching staff and the students could consider the season one that could be built upon for the future.

Supporters hoped that with many players returning for the fall of 1934, Scott could continue to produce a team capable of competing successfully. Clinton Walker, the captain of the 1933 squad, stayed as a line coach. Rhea Walker, Captain Clarence "Sugar" Forehand, Johnny Small, Dick Dozier and two or three others from the 1933 squad showed up, but Elmo Barnes and several others expected to return failed to appear. Newcomer Fred Kyle did well both in football and as a hurdler on the track team. Frank "Bumpy" Valentine, the former Commodore who had played the previous year for Augusta Military Academy, added some weight at fullback, and he could throw the ball for distance. Scott planned to switch Bob Richardson from the backfield to the forward wall.

However, fans found out just how weak the club was when it faced the Potomac State Catamounts before 500 fans at Larchmont Field. Scott's lads lost this brutal battle, as the visitors took advantage of the weight differential, their line averaging some 180 pounds. A driving rain thwarted the passing attack. Towering Potomac tackles easily crashed through the Division line, throwing Brave backs for losses time and again. The ground game of the vaunted visitors, along with well-timed laterals, ate up chunks of yardage. Finally, in the fourth quarter, Dick Dozier was able to feed a pass to Fred Kyle, and Valentine spiraled one to Heyward Mercer for Norfolk's lone score in a 32-6 loss.[12]

In the next game, Scott took his men out to Norfolk's Naval Training Station, where the "Boots" had just organized their team. Some 1,500, mostly military personnel, watched their talented but unpracticed club battle evenly against the visitors for three quarters and then score in the final quarter. Played in the middle of the week, the game was more of a scrimmage, as Scott tried out some new lineups in preparation for Friday's upcoming game at Louisburg. Indeed, the afternoon daily labeled the visitors the Norfolk Division College of William & Mary-VPI "Reserves," but the starting lineup bore a striking resemblance to the usual eleven, so it seems best to count the defeat.[13]

After this loss, the Louisburg Trojans swamped the Braves, 45-0 in North Carolina, with 20 first downs against four for Scott's men. According to punt returner Rhea Walker, the field at Louisburg was on so much of a slope that in fielding a punt, he would observe the ball over the horizon well before seeing onrushing linemen.

As might be expected, the Braves came away from Louisburg with many injuries, including a few serious ones—along with a 0-3 record. In an attempt to find a winning combination, the Division once again went to the Naval Station, this time just for a scrimmage. Finally, as October ended, the Division won its first game, besting South Norfolk High School by scoring twice in the second half at the Larchmont Field. Enjoying a weight advantage for the first time all season, the Braves overcame the scrappy Tigers, 14-0.[14]

In a return match with the Cape Charles Athletic Club on the Division campus before 500 fans, Scott gave Singleton Garrett a chance at quarterback again. He, along with tackle Quincy Davis and guard J. Davis, but mostly Dick Dozier at fullback "flipping passes straight as an arrow," overwhelmed the visitors, 39-0. Billy McMillan, Dick Dozier, Singleton Garrett, and Skinny Abbott all scored touchdowns in the final stanza, to go along with Elwood Brock's reception of a Dozier pass in the first quarter. Ira Richardson "played a wide-awake game at guard." The afternoon daily announced: "Entire Student Body Happy over Braves Impressive Victory." The players walked into classes on Monday with their chins "perked in the air like generals," at least as described tongue-in-cheek by reporter Harry Postove.[15]

Buoyed by the recent wins, the Braves scrimmaged with Maury, as they prepared to take on their biggest rival—the freshmen of the parent college. Again playing at Larchmont, the Braves put up a stout fight but were no match for the Papooses, particularly in the latter stages of the contest. Only Valentine received individual credit among the Braves in the local press, his punting being one of the "outstanding features of the game." Given that the William & Mary frosh eleven had beaten Louisburg by three touchdowns and Norfolk had lost to the same team by 45 points, one would have to consider the 18-0 loss at Larchmont no great stain. The Williamsburg paper praised the Division's Captain Forehand and "Red" Simmons for their work in stopping runners in the first half. A Bill Miller interception also helped keep the contest scoreless until the second half. The "Norfolk Braves put up a determined resistance in the first half and prevented the mighty Ducs (another name for freshmen on the Williamsburg campus) from gaining."[16]

The weekend before Thanksgiving, the Division played its last game of the season. This game would have been a cakewalk for any of Scott's earlier teams, as Hopewell High School had recently lost to Wilson High by three touchdowns. Moreover, the Hopewell coach thought the game was scheduled for Saturday afternoon and did not learn of the 3 o'clock Friday afternoon starting time until noon that same day. Because they did not reach Norfolk until well after the startup time, the Black Devils had to forego any warm-ups. Taking advantage of their opponent's stiffness, Norfolk rolled to a quick touchdown, with halfback Fred Johnson scoring from 11 yards out on an off-tackle play. But Hopewell quickly rebounded to tie the game, 7-7. That proved to be the ending score. Toward the end of the game, Rhea Walker informs us, those who owned autos lined them up next to the field and put on the headlights to allow completion of the contest. A losing season (2 wins, 4 losses, 1 tie) had come to an end. The program seemed to be going downhill, quite unlike Roosevelt's New Deal.[17]

The 1935 season produced a much more positive result—indeed, the best ever for the Division football program. Two Maury High School regulars—Jimmy Stewart and Tom Hogan—matriculated and came to the Division. Equally important, Elmo Barnes, after a year's absence, returned to take a place in the backfield. Roger Denny looked solid in the line. On the negative side, Fred Edmonds, "a fast, shifty back," looked good until felled by an attack of appendicitis. Scott's hopes diminished some when Courtney Bell got a job with the Norfolk and Western Railroad and tackle Quincy C. Davis Jr. re-injured his knee.

With several experienced players returning, Scott had Billy Miller and Johnny Davis as centers, Fred Kyle at end, Ira J. Richardson at guard and Ace Mercer at end. Jack Coppedge out of Wilson High and Woody Barnes, from Oceana, also had chances of playing. Injury-prone Dick Dozier, with another year's experience, looked ready for greater success, now being designated the club's captain. Buck Miles returned to help train the linemen. Nothing much was expected from 10 scrubs.

After the usual scrimmage between Maury High and the Braves, a crowd of 3,500 at the Navy Base watched the Division carry a close game against the Boots, with Singleton Garrett and Fred Kyle scoring touchdowns, the former on a run and the latter on a pass. The Braves had defeated recruits that had a weight advantage averaging some 15 pounds. The 13-10 triumph, compared to the 6-0 loss the previous season, set a positive tone for the entire season.[18]

Seeking revenge, Scott's men took on the powerful Louisburg Junior College eleven, the same team that had humiliated them the two previous years. In the game's first quarter at Larchmont Field, the Braves carried out a sustained 80-yard drive, with Dozier tossing to Barnes for 20 yards and Tom Hogan passing to Dozier for another 10. Hogan then hit the center of the enemy line for the first touchdown. Dozier kicked the extra point. Norfolk's defense dominated the entire game. In the second quarter, center Earl Jackson, who had intercepted a critical pass in the game against the Boots, grabbed a fumble on the visitors' 25 yard line. Tom Hogan ran for 16 yards and Barnes capped the short drive with a goal-crossing run. Once again, Dozier put the ball between the uprights for the extra point. For the first time in its history the Division looked as if it had a reliable drop kicker.[19]

The next game was played at Keyser, West Virginia against Potomac State, a team that had also beaten Norfolk in the past. The Braves dominated the game against a penalty-plagued home team, but they were fortunate to come away with a 13-7 win. Tom Hogan rushed for two touchdowns. Dozier made one extra point but missed the other, and he also missed three field-goal attempts, giving the home eleven a chance to pull out the game. With time running out, however, an illegal substitution stopped the threat.[20]

An overconfident contingent of Braves had a hard time getting an initial score against South Norfolk High School in a game at Cascade Park, a new stadium built with funds from the Public Works Administration. But after being stopped two times within the home club's 5-yard line, Hogan's running and Dozier's passing allowed the visitors to break through. Held to but two touchdowns in the first three quarters, the Braves, with what writer Tom Fergusson called "the fury of a coastal storm," battered the home team with three more scores in the final stanza. In the game's highlight, Elmo Barnes passed to Woody Barnes for 40 yards in the air. At the end, Norfolk came away with a 33-0 win. The public soon found out why Woody Barnes had replaced Jimmy Stewart at end. Stewart, a 1933 All State selection from Maury, had found a job in the improving economy.[21]

With four straight wins, the Braves returned to Bain Field to face the Blues of Gallaudet College. That institution for the deaf had built quite a reputation for its football prowess over the years, but it was no match for the Norfolk Division, which scored in every quarter. The Braves employed about every device, according to Fergusson—"power plays, tricky laterals, and a dazzling overhead attack." Fullback Jack Coppedge scored on a 1-yard plunge and caught at least two passes from Captain Dozier. The only negative aspect of the game was Dozier's failure in four of five extra-point attempts, due to leg injury he was nursing.[22]

Despite their winning ways, the Braves figured to have a hard time in their biggest game of the year—against the freshmen of the parent school. William & Mary had walloped Louisburg by far more than Norfolk had earlier that season. But despite playing poorly, the Braves captured their sixth straight win when Dozier led a 75-yard drive in the third period. Sitting on the 5-yard line, the Division needed four downs to score the touchdown, finally accomplished by Hogan on a plunge. A Dozier-to-Kyle pass gave Norfolk an extra point. That odd score, 7-4, came about because of two Norfolk safeties, one when center Earl Jackson hiked the ball over Hogan's head and out of the end zone. Fumbles on both sides kept the two offenses at bay. A small crowd showed up for the Friday afternoon battle.[23]

In the middle of November, the Norfolk Division took on a new rival—East Carolina Teachers College—at Trucker Stadium in Portsmouth. That Friday afternoon, a small crowd watched one of the most hard-fought struggles of the season. In the second quarter, a 15-yard penalty against the Braves put the ball on their 2-yard line. As described by Fergusson, "the Division warriors hurled themselves with might and main at the plunging thrusts of two powerful backs and held for three straight plays," but on fourth down, "Hoot" Gibson took a lateral and crossed the chalk. The Braves then traveled 88 yards, as Barnes and Hogan traded gains. Hogan then took a pass from Barnes and ran 40 yards for the score. Neither team scored on extra points, but ECTC secured safeties on two bad passes from center Jackson. The Teachers only needed one to win the game. The press partially attributed the 10-6 loss to an injury to Captain Dozier, which kept him out of most of the game.[24]

Even though he was not expected to play against Hopewell in the next game, Dozier kicked four extra points in addition to either two or three touchdowns he scored (the campus paper gave him two; the morning daily three). The score of the game against Hopewell High on the road was either 34-0 or 34-2. Scott shifted Earl Jackson from center to halfback. In strategizing before the game, Scott planned to use Coppedge in the backfield with the intent of letting him do some passing. Ace Mercer was supposed to replace the injured Dozier.[25]

The lopsided victory over Hopewell, the club that had tied them at home the year before, should have brought the season to an end, but Scott told his players to take a few days off and return to practice the day after Thanksgiving. On December 7, the Braves returned to where they had started the season—the Naval Station—to play the Boots, this time the gate receipts to go to Navy Relief. Some 2,500 showed up to watch what should have been a very close encounter, given the result of the first game, and the improvement of the "Recruits." But with a more or less healthy Dozier providing versatility, Tom Hogan running and punting well, Elmo Barnes catching and running, Woody Barnes catching passes and Roger Denny playing outstanding defense, the collegians rolled to a 21-7 triumph. With its 8 and 1 record, and with wins against the Navy Base bracketing the season, the junior college enjoyed its best football season ever.[26]

In partial recognition for the successful season and some six years of Division football, Scott announced his all-time, all-star team. The campus newspaper printed photos of seven of the men Scott chose: Elmo Barnes, Mike Cavish, Dick Dozier, Tommy Nee, Jack Saunders, Johnny Singleton and Clinton Walker. Scott picked Cavish as his best utility man. Other initial sections included Frank Jackson, the diminutive guard; Fred Kyle; Courtney Bell, likely the fastest back "ever to wear the Green," in the estimation of the reporter; Terry Maxey, quarterback of the 1931 club; and Jim Burton, also of the class of '31. An alternate or second-team line consisted of ends Harry Ball, '32, and Heywood Mercer, tackles Roger Denny and Lloyd Patrick, guards Johnny Doyle and Louis Carner, and center Earl Jackson. The backfield featured Tom Hogan and Junie Wilson at halfback, Billy Morgan at quarterback, and Jack Hawkins at fullback. Scott designated Saunders White as the best alternate utility.

A year later another list of Scott's favorites appeared in the campus paper, again described as a "Six-Year Sports History." In addition to some of the names on the original list, the new list added "Buck" Bowen, Bill Eames, Clarence Forehand, Walter Lakin and Earl Martin. There is no way to determine which of these composed his real all-star eleven.[27]

In the wake of the football club's 1935 success, Norfolk Division students found athletes playing a more prominent role on campus. The editor of the campus paper, like his predecessors, clearly had an agenda regarding the student athletic fee. A student vote, although yielding a poor turnout, indicated that quite a few students wanted to put more emphasis on intramurals and less on competition against other schools. But in the spring elections for the Men's Student Government Association that year, Fred Edmonds, Fred Kyle and Dick Dozier, all of whom participated in at least two sports, carried three of the five most important positions. Later in May, the outgoing editor of the newspaper recommended Dick Dozier as his replacement.

Wilson "Dick" Dozier

Before taking over as school newspaper editor, Wilson "Dick" Dozier wrote a letter in which he questioned whether many students whose classes ended early in the day would stick around for late-afternoon intramural contests. Dozier's editorials over the next year dealt with numerous issues, but as might be expected, he wrote extensively on the role of collegiate athletics. In one of his editorials, he argued that sports should be given the same consideration as any other department. Athletes did not want special favors, only recognition that mind and body should grow together. He also deplored the win-at-any-cost notion that pervaded major collegiate sports. In another editorial, he contended that those who played football in college found pleasure in playing the game because doing so released emotions "smoldering in their natures, emotions that must be given expression. College men do not, as a rule, play football to learn a life's business, or even to develop their bodies; they play because of the pure pleasure derivable from the game." Just as musicians, poets or painters found pleasure in doing what they did as an "outlet for emotional expression," so, too, did athletes. Pleasure for both artists and athletes came from doing well.[28]

In another editorial, Dozier expressed displeasure of the treatment of Eugenia Berry, the lone cheerleader, who had left the school, possibly because students had subjected her to "unjustified ridicule because of her unusually great enthusiasm in cheer leading." It may well be that the Division students had not quite accepted the idea of having female cheerleaders, even though the upper South did lead the way in having women cheer at football games in the 1930s. Through the Progressive Era, women had been pretty much confined to the stands, a practice perhaps reflecting the male fear of what some called the "New American Woman." Dozier thought Berry's "unbalanced enthusiasm" contrasted rather sharply with the "dull lethargy of our present student body." He hoped that one or more of the fraternities might organize the cheering or that the campus clubs (fraternities) could organize a joint committee to that end, "not so much for the football team, but for the College." A few years later a squad of females served as basketball cheerleaders for the Division, but they apparently never led cheers as a group at the football games.[29]

Wilson "Dick" Dozier was a man of letters both athletic and written. From 1933 to 1935, Dozier excelled in football, baseball and basketball. He also excelled in the classroom, even serving as editor for the school newspaper. On the football field, the handsome and energetic Dozier played both halfback and quarterback positions for the Braves. Immensely popular with his teammates, he was honored by being chosen team captain for the 1935 season. In 1936, he transferred to the College of William & Mary and played for the Indians. On August 13, 1945, two days before the Japanese surrendered, Dozier made the ultimate sacrifice when he was killed in action while serving for the military. (Courtesy of Sargeant Memorial Room, Norfolk Public Library)

This 1933 photograph shows coach Tommy Scott (middle) drawing a play during practice. Scott is surrounded by members of his team as well as team captain, Clinton Walker (kneeling on left), and assistant coach, Buck Miles (kneeling on right). (Courtesy of Sargeant Memorial Room, Norfolk Public Library)

Looking through the legs of center Billy Miller, this photograph shows the 1933 Division backfield. From left to right are Dick Dozier, Elmo Barnes, Joe Redford and Rhea Walker. (Courtesy of Sargeant Memorial Room, Norfolk Public Library)

On October 31, 1933, the Norfolk Division played the Tigers of South Norfolk High School at Bain Field. The Braves tamed the Tigers, winning 21-6 with Johnny Singleton scoring two touchdowns and kicking an extra point. (Courtesy of Sargeant Memorial Room, Norfolk Public Library)

Members of the school's backfield from left to right are Fred Johnson, Rhea Walker, Frank "Bumpy" Valentine and Courtney Bell. That year, the team could only muster a record of two wins, four losses and one tie. (Courtesy of Sargeant Memorial Room, Norfolk Public Library)

The line for the 1934 Braves consisted of (left to right) Heywood Mercer, left end; John Small, left tackle; Captain Clarence Forehand, left guard; Billy Miller, center; John Creech, right guard; Meryl Simmons, right tackle; and Fred Kyle, right end. (Courtesy of Sargeant Memorial Room, Norfolk Public Library)

On November 9, 1934, the Norfolk Division took on the William & Mary freshmen at Larchmont Field. The Braves would succumb to a much more talented team, 18–0. (Courtesy of Sargeant Memorial Room, Norfolk Public Library)

With four straight wins under their belt, the 1935 Braves take on the Blues of Gallaudet College at Bain Field. Here, Elmo Barnes runs the ball for the Braves. (Courtesy of Sargeant Memorial Room, Norfolk Public Library)

Dick Dozier is tackled after a gain in the Gallaudet game. (Courtesy of Sargeant Memorial Room, Norfolk Public Library)

Norfolk Division center Billy Miller looks at the camera in this unique perspective. Miller was a mainstay at the pivot position for the Braves from 1933 to 1936. His steady play would earn him selection as team captain for the 1936 season. (Courtesy of Sargeant Memorial Room, Norfolk Public Library)

From 1933 to 1935, Elmo Barnes would play quarterback for the Division. A speedy and great open-field runner, this Emporia, Virginia native was known as the "Emporia Flash." (Courtesy of Sargeant Memorial Room, Norfolk Public Library)

CHAPTER FOUR

The New Deal Lends a Hand

Although the club's successful 1935 season doubtless raised some eyebrows, the big news of that year was the decision of the college's Board of Visitors and the Norfolk City Council to have a stadium built on the campus. A. Herbert Foreman, who also served on the Norfolk Board of Education, went before the council to acquire the acreage on which the school had an option to purchase for $14,000. The federal government had already granted funds under the Public Works Agency for the soon-to-be-completed administration building, which occupied the site of the old football field. That facility, constructed with the help of the PWA, included two gymnasiums, one for men and the other for women, with the women's gym located on a large stage. For such a small school, the Division was about to have lots of athletic amenities.

In 1933, the first year of the New Deal, the city sought $140,000 from the PWA, but when that agency could not come up with any money for a football facility, the college estimated it could raise little more than $12,000. Foreman first thought in terms of a facility to hold about 6,000, but which could be added to over time. The college's board asked the city to approach the federal government for a $250,000 loan to build a "modern plant." Sports columnist Bill Cox of *The Virginian-Pilot* urged everyone to get behind a proposed 15,000-seat facility. In January 1934, Foreman convinced the city council to cooperate with the College of William & Mary's plan to build a stadium, a gym and a classroom building with $250,000 in PWA money. The Association of Commerce, the Tidewater Automobile Association, the Retail Merchants Association, and the Real Estate Board all passed resolutions in support of the plan. Federal officials, however, balked at the idea of including a stadium but did agree to help fund the classroom building and the gymnasium for $100,000. The PWA later came through with funds to add a swimming pool to the facility.[1]

As planning proceeded for constructing the campus building, Foreman and college leaders again sought help in building the proposed stadium. In June 1935, the city council agreed to a scheme for a larger stadium, using a trust fund to help the financing. The city would buy land, turn it over to the college, and receive payments over time to cover the cost.

Architect Clarence A. Neff had already drawn up a sketch of the future facility that was published in the local newspaper, along with information that the Emergency Relief Administration would grant the college $78,081.55 to help construct the first phase. The city would loan the college $24,000, to be repaid from stadium earnings. Private donors pledged about $6,000 to keep the project alive as negotiations continued with the federal government.

Around the same time, the Roosevelt administration, still combating the Depression with what came to be called the "Second New Deal," persuaded Congress to put much of the relief and recovery programs into a giant organization known as the Works Progress Administration. Aware of this change, in September 1935, Foreman convinced the Norfolk City Council to have the city manager, under emergency provisions in the 1918 charter, apply to the Works Progress Administration for enough funds to complete a stadium holding more than 17,000. Congressman Colgate Darden later claimed that President Roosevelt, through the influence of a Foreman connection in Washington, D.C., put the project on the fast track.[2]

Tracing the financing of this enterprise is nearly impossible if one relies on newspaper accounts. One set of numbers has about $90,000 coming from the federal government with the college chipping in just over $6,000 for the classroom building. Later, the newspapers calculated that counting the new classroom building as well as the stadium, the federal government kicked in almost $280,000 while William & Mary came up with over $106,000 and the city of Norfolk some $16,000. The total outlay reached over $400,000, including about $35,000 from the WPA and over $4,500 from the college for campus beautification. However, when summarized later in an editorial, the federal government had given $268,000 and had loaned $86,000 on a 20-year 4-percent loan to the city. The federal government loaned this money to the city, but at some point the college attained ownership of not only the classroom building, but the stadium as well. Another editorial the following year summarized the numbers to read $125,000 for the classroom and $300,000 for the stadium. Whatever the numbers, the editor praised the projects. He noted that the "Depression is on the way out," helped by the college and an annual payroll of $50,000 that went to 20 faculty members serving 405 students.[3]

Landscaping included a decorative serpentine brick wall around the eastern edge of the campus. Construction of Foreman Field also required extensive work on Bluestone Avenue. The campus' architectural style and landscaping was modeled on Colonial Williamsburg, which was being re-created largely through the largesse of the Rockefeller family. Director Walter Hodges based the new classroom building on Bruton Parish Church, with which, as a former administrator on the Williamsburg campus, he was quite familiar. Although he was satisfied with most of Hodges's work, the president of the College of William & Mary praised the landscaping but lamented the library's low quantity of books.

Much of the land on the south end of the field where the stadium was built consisted of a swamp. Indeed, a drainage ditch extended along the south end of the campus on 49th Street. Filling in the swamp required numerous loads of dirt, not only before the building's construction, but also later, when the terrain settled. The federal government paid for some of this work carried out after 1936.

City fathers called for a new high school to be located on Larchmont Elementary School's spacious grounds, which included quite a bit of marshland. Authorities envisioned fields for soccer, hockey and baseball gracing the Larchmont site. The city of Norfolk originally asked the federal government for $500,000 for that project but was turned down because the plan did not spend enough money. Once funding was secured in a later proposal, it was decided to build the new federally funded high school on Granby Street, on what was then the east side of the city. Tennis courts were already or would soon be in place southeast of Larchmont Elementary School.

Around the same time that the Norfolk Division built its new classroom building, a new concrete and steel bridge was built over the Lafayette River on Hampton Boulevard, thanks to PWA funds. Norfolk's northern suburbs were certainly major beneficiaries of the New Deal.[4]

When the classroom building was under construction, Dick Dozier and another player, according to Rhea Walker, were among the workers. As the two were working on the girders for 30 hours a week for $18, a fellow worker kept raining tobacco juice on them. The next day, Dozier came to work with his own plug of tobacco, and finding the proper perch, returned the favor.[5]

While the 1935 Braves played their fall season at Bain Field, work commenced on the stadium, with completion projected for the next fall. All that fall and winter, workers who were probably paid minimum wage poured concrete and cleaned and laid old bricks taken from buildings razed elsewhere in the city. In December, the campus newspaper fumed about the city government's and college administration's decision not to let the Division team christen the field by playing the first game in it. The parent school and the University of Virginia would do the honors the first week in October, 1936. The Sunday editor of *The Virginian-Pilot*, R. K. T. "Kit" Larson, suggested that the Division should play earlier the same day, with the extension game being a warm-up for the big match between the more prestigious institutions, but nothing came of that suggestion.[6]

In September 1936, just as seats were being installed in the two parts of the stadium, another hurricane came up the coast. High water levels downtown came within a foot of the record 1933 storm. Ocean View and Willoughby Spit absorbed a beating, but no one died this time because residents had been warned to evacuate. Officials feared that the storm meant that the stadium wouldn't be available for the William & Mary-University of Virginia game, but contractors had the stadium ready, and the work had to have impressed those who attended games at Bain Field. Primarily a football and track facility, the west and east stands stood symmetrically opposite each other, each holding close to 9,000 seats. The stadium even had lights.[7]

Why the city and college had not built an all-purpose stadium is not clear. In that same decade, several councilmen expressed concern about the legality of city ownership of property that might be rented out to a professional baseball team. These councilmen seemed oblivious to the fact that the city already owned municipal golf courses that were routinely rented out to private individuals. It may well be that they did not want to encourage the New York Yankees, who now ran the Norfolk farm team, to think Norfolk might be willing to subsidize the local Tars. In 1940, when Bain Field had to be replaced, the city sold its land at the old Lafayette Field to a nonprofit group of concerned citizens, who then built a stadium and rented it to the Yankees. In that same year, the city of Portsmouth built a modern outdoor arena, making it serviceable for all kinds of sports, including the professional baseball team. Thus, Portsmouth ended up with an all-purpose facility that later became known as Frank D. Lawrence Stadium. The reluctance of Norfolk's City Council members to have the city own a stadium may help to explain why, although the city incurred some debt to help build Foreman Field, it refused to stake any claim to ownership.

Some 15,000 sweltering fans showed up for the dedication and inaugural game at Foreman Field. Some said it was the biggest crowd ever to see a football game in Virginia, but they apparently did not know that at least an equal number had attended a collegiate contest in Richmond years before World War I. Guests included President John Stewart Bryan of the College of William & Mary, Virginia Governor George C. Perry, Norfolk Mayor W. R. L. Taylor and a host of other dignitaries.

Although William & Mary and the University of Virginia were certainly appropriate teams to play in a dedication game for the new field, their football programs were in a transitory condition at the time. The University of Virginia had experienced a disastrous season in 1935, with four scoreless ties against the likes of Hampden-Sydney and William & Mary and a disastrous showing against archrival North Carolina. The school then left the Southern Conference over the issue of scholarship aid. Many members of the conference had been giving out such aid to student athletes surreptitiously; Virginia insisted on continuing to extend financial assistance, but without any cover up. Branch Bocock, who had coached in several colleges much earlier in the century, including Virginia Tech and the University of North Carolina, had started coaching at Williamsburg in the late 1920s. After taking time off to help restore Colonial Williamsburg, he returned to coaching at the college in hopes of making the football program equal to any in the state. When the game went to Virginia, 7-0, the Indians would have to wait four more years for their first victory ever over the Cavaliers.

Although press coverage of this contest virtually submerged interest in the first game of the season for the Braves, Division folks could all take pride in Dick Dozier's punt returns and hard-nosed defense on behalf of the parent eleven. In addition, both Fred Kyle and Singleton Garrett were on the William & Mary roster.[8]

Kyle got a chance to play for the Indians at Foreman Field later that year in a game against William & Mary, who had lost by a touchdown to the Generals of Washington and Lee, which at the time had the best record of any of Virginia's major colleges. Only 3,000 showed up that day, a rather disappointing number for such a huge stadium. The low turnout proved to be an enduring concern for those who had urged the creation of such a large facility. Despite the presence of one of the best-looking football semi-ovals in the nation, Norfolk's business interests still had difficulty attracting major college games—even those between regional institutions. Even Virginia Tech battles with North Carolina clubs only drew around 6,000. Attendance reached a new low in October 1937, when only 2,851 (the number emphasized by the afternoon daily), paid to see Virginia Military Institute win an exciting game over William & Mary in "perfect weather."

The disappointed booking agent for the occasion, apparently representing the Chamber of Commerce, was none other than Walter E. "Beef" Hoffman, one of the judges on the federal district court, who ordered the integration of Norfolk's public schools in 1958, and the judge involved in the legal deal that allowed Vice President Spiro Agnew to avoid jail time by resigning his office. In addition to his duties as a ticket seller, Hoffman refereed football games, including one in 1937 between the Division and ECTC at Foreman Field. His name routinely appears in coverage of Southern Conference games.

In the summer of 1938, Norfolk's mayor and William & Mary's president appointed a committee of leading citizens to find ways to increase the facility's use. A newspaper reporter, who doubted much would come from their deliberations, pointed out that many cities, such as Baltimore, had similar "white elephants." Even at major football universities, such places only had big crowds four or five times a year. The history of Norfolk strongly suggested that pageants, outdoor theater, professional tennis and even religious revivals, like the one carried out by the great Billy Sunday in January 1920, rarely, if ever, had attracted crowds that would fill Foreman Field.

After about two years of poor attendance, a writer calling himself "a football fan" wrote to Charles Reilly, the evening daily's sports columnist. Reilly knew the man as a professional, but agreed not to divulge his name. The writer said that in passing by Foreman Field on his way to Bain Field to watch the Norfolk Shamrocks play games on Sunday, he felt, and was sure thousands of others felt the same way, "cheated" that tax funds had been used to build the "beautiful stadium," and that it was so underutilized. He knew that the owner of the Shamrocks, Harry Howren, would "pay handsomely" to play there, and if Dean Hodges and Foreman could not come to terms with him, then the city council should step in. The writer claimed that none of his Larchmont neighbors had ever expressed opposition to such games.[9]

The next fall another fan thought Norfolk's city manager and the president of William & Mary were not allowing football games on Sunday because state law would not permit Sabbath playing on state facilities. If such were the case, the writer urged legislators to change the law. He also thought it was bad enough that Norfolk lacked a respectable baseball field, but to possess a "first-class establishment" for football, but not use it on Sundays violated taxpayers' rights. Reilly noted that in response to an inquiry about using the site for a charity game, President John Stewart Bryan of the College of William & Mary claimed that state ownership of Foreman and his interpretation of state law meant that he could not make the field available on Sundays.[10]

The issue of Sunday activities had a history dating back to colonial times. In 1877, when it became clear that the "blue laws" could not pass judicial scrutiny because of the "wall of separation" between church and state, the Virginia legislature turned to a labor law to keep businesses closed on the Christian Sabbath. That law was also used to prevent professional baseball players from earning money on Sundays. But in 1934, as part of a tidal wave of social liberalism that accompanied the New Deal, Virginia opened up state liquor stores (in the wake of the rescinding of the 18th Amendment), and the Virginia Court of Appeals overturned the injunction against professional baseball on Sundays. Around the same time, the legislature made prize fighting legal and it came within a whisker of allowing gambling at horse races. Many Norfolk residents viewed Bryan's efforts to keep professional football players off Foreman Field on Sunday as an anachronism.

Even though no professional games took place at Foreman Field through 1939, attendance did pick up quite a bit when three collegiate contests took place there that year. A VPI-UNC encounter came close to bringing in 10,000 spectators, a number short of the 13,000 projected sales, but the man in charge of ticket sales, Tom Scott, was happy with the turnout. The University of Virginia-William & Mary repeat of 1936, with Division alums George Harper and Bill Turville on the Indian roster, attracted only 7,500. An even smaller crowd came to the VMI-Maryland game. Maury High and newcomer Granby High School, with its first football program in 1939, sometimes drew a few thousand on Friday nights or Saturday afternoons. So if Foreman Field could be made available for every other Sunday afternoon, one could make a case that at least during the fall, effective use was being made of the facility.

Playing in the Dixie Pro Football League, the Shamrocks took on teams like the Richmond Arrows or the Charlotte Clippers. In those years the Norfolk Tars, a semi-pro club, played in the Virginia-Carolina League. The local press occasionally mentioned former Division players among the professional or semi-professional clubs. Billy Morgan, one of the original Braves, had his same picture appear in the newspaper nearly every year, as the sparkplug for the South Norfolk Aces or the Berkley Bears. In 1939, he played quarterback for a weak Shamrock eleven. Tom Hogan, who played for the Division in 1935, performed well in one of the Shamrocks' early losses. In 1938, Claiborne Nixon, who played for the Division in 1936, led the Elizabeth City Cardinals into Bain to take on one of the local semi-pro clubs. Around the same time, Elmo Barnes showed up in a newspaper photo wearing the apparel of the Portsmouth Cubs.

In the fall of 1940, the Shamrocks played most of their games at the so-called "new park." Later known as High Rock Park and still later as Myers Field, it was located on the site of the former Lafayette Field. With Tommy Scott coaching them, they got off to a poor start, even though George Stirnweiss, one of the University of North Carolina's greatest backs, joined after the season started. Only when the owner secured the services of broken-field-runner John Zontini, a veteran of the Dixie Pro League, did the 1940 season turn around for the Norfolk club, by which point an ailing Scott no longer was at the helm. And even though the Shamrocks helped out finances at Foreman Field by paying to practice there on week nights, they did not play games there on Sundays.

Attendance for most Division games never exceeded 3,000, and sometimes the Braves were fortunate to find a few hundred in the stands. The 1938 edition drew 500 or fewer for most of its games. Except for an occasional Thanksgiving high school game and a few boxing matches, most crowds for athletic contests rattled around the place. The facility seemed to defy the axiom that nature abhors a vacuum. The local press frequently editorialized about the situation, noting the area's geographical isolation, the state's lack of nationally renowned football powers, and the high price for tickets given the weak local market. One editorial explained the lack of interest as part of a "Virginia spirit" that was "as complacent toward athletics as it is toward politics."[11]

Finally, early in the 1940 season, a match sponsored by Norfolk's Junior Chamber of Commerce between William & Mary and North Carolina State, won by the latter in an upset over "fearless" Jimmy Howard and the Tribe, drew a record crowd of 17,500. Navy personnel, many of whom were now converging on the area due to the military buildup in response to the deterioration in world affairs, received reduced rates to attend. The inclination of the sailors to find better seating led to a near breakdown of relations between servicemen and civilians. A few William & Mary students also sat in the wrong seats and had to be removed by officials with the help of some Navy men. In the middle of this imbroglio was none other than Tommy Scott. Hodges apologized profusely for himself, Scott and A. Lee Smith (who handled logistics for the game), at a meeting of civic leaders who were trying to assess blame for the situation. Tom Hanes, managing editor of the afternoon daily, was willing to accept the apology, but at least one outspoken critic who attended the session viewed such absolution as a "whitewash." The press pretty much excluded from criticism the 1,800 sailors (rumors hinted at alcohol consumption) who sat in the wrong seats and Police Chief John F. Woods, who refused to send his officers into the stands to remove them. Chief blame then rested on the shoulders of Foreman Field management for not providing enough ushers to handle the much bigger-than-expected crowd. The next collegiate contest, a Tech upset of Virginia, brought in but 10,000 customers. Given the greater popularity of that contest, one can only assume Uncle Sam's sailors did not buy cheaper tickets. But officials at VPI were upset that income from program sales went to the Norfolk Division athletic fund. By that point, Scott was so beset by both administrative and health problems that he likely had little role in management.[12]

Students seemed not to worry about the use of Foreman Field, but a student editor had complained about another New Deal program—the Federal Emergency Relief Administration. His particular grievance related to the part of the program that helped pay college tuition in return for work on campus by the recipient. This form of work-study apparently produced a lot of busy work, such as less-than-knowledgeable students grading objective tests several times just to build up their work time. Moreover, some students, if one is to believe a campus editorial, really did not need to have their tuition paid, and instead used the money to take vacations in Florida. If Division football players did not receive such aid under FERA, several certainly did later from the National Youth Administration, which carried on a similar program. The principal problem with such aid is that it required time and effort from students taking a full load of courses and practicing football nearly every day.[13]

This circa 1935 photograph shows the new academic building and gymnasiums, one for men and one for women. The facility was constructed with the help of the PWA. (Courtesy of Special Collections and University Archives, Perry Library, Old Dominion University)

This 1935 photograph shows the campus landscaping, including a decorative serpentine brick wall. The old academic building can be seen in the background. (Courtesy of Special Collections and University Archives, Perry Library, Old Dominion University)

While the 1935 Braves played their fall season at Bain Field, work commenced on a new stadium built largely with old bricks taken from razed buildings throughout the city. This 1935 photograph shows the progress on the city's new stadium. (Courtesy of Sargeant Memorial Room, Norfolk Public Library)

This circa 1940 image shows the new Foreman Field and new academic building only a few years after completion. The growth of the neighborhood around the stadium is clearly evident. (Courtesy of Special Collections and University Archives, Perry Library, Old Dominion University)

Governor George C. Perry addresses the crowd at the dedication of Foreman Field on October 3, 1936. (Courtesy of Special Collections and University Archives, Perry Library, Old Dominion University)

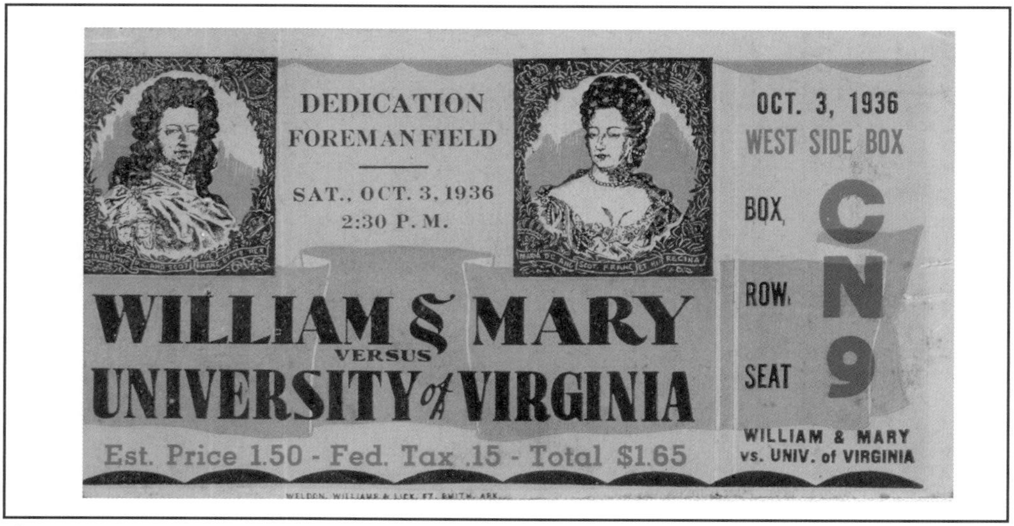

This ticket gained admission to a box seat at Foreman Field's inaugural game between the College of William & Mary and the University of Virginia. More than 15,000 fans attended the dedication and game. (Courtesy of Special Collections and University Archives, Perry Library, Old Dominion University)

CHAPTER FIVE

Division Football Holds On, 1936–1938

The year Foreman Field was built (1936), the Division football agenda included the usual schedule, despite many holes to fill in the lineup. Scott had lost his entire backfield and several linemen. Scott thought Jimmy Stewart would return and Lonny Seay, the great punter for Maury, would join the team. But neither Scholastic All-Stater came to the first official practice. An off year would certainly be expected by those who knew much about the available talent. Ben Dodge, a former Maury All-State selection and a Hokie, would coach the line.

In a scrimmage with Maury, Billy Miller and Maury Riganto showed up well at center, but Johnny Doyle, the expected new quarterback, had been kicked in the head in a prior scrimmage with the Navy Yard Marines. Scott decided to go with speedy Freddy Edmonds at quarterback and move Doyle to halfback once he recovered. Frank Jackson, "the greatest little guard to matriculate at the Larchmont institution," broke his arm in three places in the same scrimmage. The Braves later added Elizabeth City's Claiborne Nixon, who had starred the previous year for the Duke freshman, and for unknown reasons, chose to compete for the Division. Preston "Ham" Mathews, who played for the VPI frosh, looked like a possible fullback.[1]

The Braves had some trouble disposing of the South Norfolk eleven at Cascade Park, but they managed to overcome what some thought was the best "B"-level scholastic team in the state, winning, 21-0. The Tigers had already lost to "A"-level Maury and Newport News High by two touchdowns in each case, so it looked as if the Division's representative that year might be slightly better than the best secondary schools. In scoring one touchdown, Scott used a play in which end Woody Barnes, a graduate of South Norfolk High, ended up throwing the ball to quarterback Fred Edmonds.

The next Friday, the Braves planned to play the first game under the lights at Foreman Field, but a rainstorm and problems with the lighting forced a postponement until Monday night. And so in the first Monday night football game ever played in Foreman Field, the Division took on its old rival—the Louisburg Trojans—before about 3,000 spectators.

After considering making Barnes his quarterback, Scott went back to Edmonds. Behind 6-0 at the half, the Braves unleashed their vaunted aerial attack when the versatile half-back Nixon threw to quarterback Edmonds to bring the ball deep into Louisburg territory. An injured Barnes, now playing halfback, scored on a run. Nixon gave the Braves the lead with a drop kick. The next time the Braves secured the oval, they scored, as Barnes once again drove over the chalk line. Although Nixon intercepted a pass on the ensuing Trojan drive, Louisburg blocked a punt and scored a safety, thus explaining the unusual score of 13-8 in the home team's favor.[2]

Despite the win, the sports editor of the campus paper complained about the lack of vocal support for the team, wondering if students thought they were too "sophisticated" to partake of pre-game rallies and the like. Did they perhaps think such behavior resembled high school? Even the best collegiate teams needed full fan support to bring out their best.[3]

Scott had arranged for another game the next Friday evening, this one against another traditional rival—Shenandoah—but the game had to be put off until Saturday afternoon after rain played havoc with the new lighting system. The visiting eleven included a forward line weighing on average about 185 pounds, with one experienced collegiate back coming in at 190, and the fullback, all 6 feet 3 inches of him, topping 240 pounds. After first deciding to use Edmonds at quarterback, Scott turned to Barnes on the day of the game. No matter who piloted the club, the Hornets proved too much. Although the Braves managed eight first downs, their only chance to score came early in the game when an interference call gave them the ball at the 6-inch line. They failed to convert, and that turned out to be the turning point, as the "heavy and aggressive line" of the visitors belatedly battered their way to 16 first downs and one touchdown. A huge fullback converted to quarterback and two smaller components of the Shenandoah eleven finally broke through in the fourth quarter. The visitors then scored a safety when Division center Nick Carter hiked the ball into the Braves' end zone. Certainly, an 8-0 loss to such a hefty rival should not be considered an embarrassment, but it did put a definite damper on the record and left the club, as might be expected, with lots of injuries.[4]

In the aftermath of the loss to Shenandoah, Edmonds supposedly quit the club and the school, and Billy Miller, the "crack" center, sustained a season-ending injury. Joe Root, who once starred for Wilson High, joined the backfield and Sid Krukin took over at center. Despite these setbacks, the Braves journeyed to Washington, D.C. to play Gallaudet. Scott's men had beaten the Blues rather handily at home the previous year, but with a less experienced lineup, the outcome of this year's contest on different turf was in great doubt until the very end. A "stubby" quarterback scored twice on line plunges for Gallaudet, giving the home team a 13-point lead. Late in the first half, substitute back Jim Padgett carried a punt return 80 yards for the first Norfolk score, and Johnny Edmonds ambled another 40 yards after catching a pass. The two big gainers brought the Braves back into a tie at halftime. Then late in the third quarter, with the ball on the Gallaudet 20-yard line, Nixon placed a ball "squarely between the uprights." With the game winding down, Nixon knelt down in the end zone, thus yielding a safety, but in effect winning the game, 16-15.[5]

The victory again left Scott with many injured players as the club headed to Greenville, North Carolina on the last day of October to take on East Carolina Teachers College. From the outset, the game did not go well for the visitors. Nixon had a hard time matching the punts of his ECTC counterpart, but the home team "completely outclassed the Norfolk boys in every division of play" and scored in every quarter. Total dominance by East Carolina produced a 25-0 loss, one of the worst margins of defeat sustained by the Division.[6]

The season stood little chance for an immediate upswing, as the Braves now took on Newport News Apprentice in the wake of news that Franklin Roosevelt had crushed Alf

Landon in the recent presidential race. Many experts expected Roosevelt to win but by a narrow margin. Similarly, no one really expected the Braves to beat the Builders, but Scott's men hoped to keep it close; however, as in politics and football, the Braves absorbed another lopsided loss, 25-0. In those times, the shipyard school had one of the better football programs in the state. Apprentice brought its 40-member band, several former Maury players, a team that outweighed the Braves by over 10 pounds on average, and a record of wins against the likes of Randolph-Macon and Hampden-Sydney. And they had little trouble disposing of the smaller, crippled Braves. After building up a lead, their coach brought in his reserves, keeping the score down.[7]

With the record now 3-3, the Braves found someone they could beat on Armistice Day when they slipped by the Boots at Foreman Field, 7-6, with the visitors scoring late in the game. Both touchdowns indirectly resulted from fumbles; Nixon's "educated toe" in securing the extra point turned out to be the difference.[8]

The next struggle pitted the Braves against the favored William & Mary Papooses, which had six Maury graduates on the club. By this point in the season, Scott's active roster had been reduced to either 12 or 13, depending on whether one could count Jim Padgett, who limped away from practice with a pulled ligament. Also during the encounter, "Ace" Mercer broke a rib. Although the Braves went "down fighting" under the lights of Foreman Field before some 2,000, the 15-0 loss could not even be considered a moral victory. The Braves might have come closer had Nixon not been ejected in the second quarter for retaliating against one of the rival team's less talented players, "One-Punch" Elmo Legg, who had continually kneed and slugged him. The campus newspaper assumed that the rumor that the coach of the Papooses had ordered Legg to behave in that fashion could not be true. That the Braves made only one first down compared to 11 for the winners suggests that even with Nixon, the Braves would have been at a disadvantage. The season-ending loss saddled the Braves with a record of four wins and four defeats.[9]

Even though odd-numbered years (1933 and 1935) had been good for the football program, it did not look as if the 1937 personnel would keep the trend going. Only 12 players showed up for the first practice: Ed Barrell, Bill (probably Woody) Barnes, John Brown, Jack Harris, Ned Howell, Gilly Lewis, Garland Lively, Joe Root, Louis Smith, Bill Tippett, Bill Turville and Eddie Tyler. Of these, only Joe Root had played the year before.

Nixon opted to move on, rather than play a second year for the Braves, but the Division traded one ex-Duke freshman for another. Walter Halme, the great Maury player of its 1935 state championship team, transferred from Duke. His performances for the Blue Imps had led a reporter to compare him to the great Ace Parker, who propelled Duke into regional domination and national prominence. Ace finished his collegiate career the same year Halme played for the Duke freshmen. In addition to Halme, Bill Rodgers, a 235-pound tackle from Oceana, showed up along with Bill Pratt, a 170-pound halfback from Elizabeth City. Johnny Edmonds, Sid Krukin and one or two others also eventually reported for duty.

The season started pretty much the way the previous season ended, with a loss, as the inexperienced Braves gave way to the powerful Apprentice club, 20-0, at Newport News. Although Norfolk completed 8 of 12 passes, but it could not cross the goal line. Every time Norfolk threatened, the Apprentice coach rushed his first string back in to hold the three-touchdown lead the home team accumulated in the first half.[10]

In the next game, this one at Foreman Field on a Friday night in late September, the Braves gave the favored University of Richmond's heavier freshmen a hard time before some 1,200 spectators. Arthur Jones, a triple-threat quarterback out of Suffolk High, completed several passes, and just as important successfully negotiated two extra points in leading the Little Spiders to a 14-13 victory. This would not be the last time his name would appear on the local sports page, as Jones became a fine varsity player for Richmond and played professional football for the Pittsburgh Steelers. Harold McVay, the Maury co-captain the previous season, helped out the winners as well. Norfolk relied on Walter Halme at fullback, Woody Barnes at quarterback and Joe Root and Bill Pratt at the halfback slots to drive the ball across the goal in the first quarter to match a Richmond touchdown. When Barnes's extra-point kick was blocked, Root picked up the ball and scored the tying point. A 35-yard pass into the end zone in the second quarter put the Baby Spiders ahead, followed by an extra point. On the ensuing kickoff, Bill Pratt returned the ball 35 yards, and then the Braves, according to Tom Fergusson, resorted to what they called "Old 97," where Barnes took the snap, and stood still as the defenders rushed him, until he heard the word "go" from Joe Root. Then he lobbed the ball over their heads to Root, who was escorted by a convoy of blockers 50 yards for the touchdown. Unfortunately, Barnes's extra-point kick was again blocked, but this time no Brave picked up the ball and ran it into the end zone. Even though the Division had fought valiantly and played reasonably well, the record stood at 0-2, and the prospects for a decent season in 1937 seemed dim.[11]

But October brought a complete turnaround. The Division started off against the Louisburg Trojans, with another revised lineup. Woody Barnes returned to end and John Brown took over at quarterback (originally Scott planned to have Joe Root give the signals). Jack Harris, who was missing half of his right arm due to a railroad accident, played right halfback. Not only did Harris play football for the Division with but one arm, he pitched successfully for the baseball team.

The first half was scoreless. Louisburg failed to take advantage of a lost Root fumble at the Division 10-yard line, and Norfolk failed three times to punch the ball across the goal from close in. But Norfolk took the second-half kickoff and took 10 plays to drive the ball into the enemy end zone, with Pratt scoring off tackle from 3 yards. Halme missed the extra point effort. In the last quarter, Brown and Pratt alternated in driving the ball to the 18-yard line where Halme passed to Brown for the score. Halme caught a pass for the extra point. The game result was even more lopsided than the 13-0 score indicated, for Louisburg had only nine first downs compared to 25 for the Braves.[12]

The next game figured to be a Division triumph as the opponent was Gallaudet, a team the Braves had beaten twice, but the previous year's win had been hard-fought and close. Jim Cooper replaced injured Sid Krukin at center. The change had little bearing on the game as Walter Halme rambled all over the place and the Braves prevailed 55-6 before 800 at Foreman Field. Halme scored three touchdowns and Bill Pratt and Joe Root chipped in two each, with Woody Barnes and Johnny Edmonds each scoring one touchdown. Jack Harris started at halfback, but although he missed out in all the scoring, his blocking helped out considerably.[13]

Fresh from their easy outing against the Blues, the Braves now faced a long-standing foe, the Hornets of Shenandoah College. The Division had won the first two games of the series, but Shenandoah had won in 1934 and 1936, no game being played when Norfolk had its dominant team in 1935. With the Maury 60-piece band playing, Woody Barnes, back at quarterback, guided a diversified attack as the Braves won, 26-0, Bill Pratt ran for three touchdowns and Walter Halme for another. All four scores indirectly resulted from interceptions by Louis Guy, Jim Knighton, Jim Cooper and Elmo Barnes. The Hornets never threatened to score and never had a chance. Norfolk's record against the husky Shenandoah men was now 3-2, as was the record for the season.[14]

Then the eleven from East Carolina Teachers College came to Foreman Field. The Teachers gave a good account of themselves even though they had not won a game all season, as one of their backs ran for 80 yards to give the visitors a 6-0 lead at the half. A crowd of only 600 watched the Friday night contest at Foreman Field as the Braves made a strong comeback in the second half. Halme and Barnes alternated carrying the ball to the 3-yard marker, from where Barnes hit Louis Smith in the end zone to tie the score. Then Johnny Edmonds scored from the 6-yard line on a reverse. Furious play by the Teachers forced some fumbles and slowed down the offense, but the Braves scored again through long gains by Halme and Barnes, with the latter taking the oval in for the last score. The Braves failed on all extra-point attempts, but they won, 18-6.[15]

Now with four wins in a row under their belts, the Braves faced the heavier freshmen of the College of William & Mary on Friday night at Foreman Field. Because they had just come from way behind to beat the Little Spiders and, earlier in the season, the Division lost narrowly to the same eleven, the Papooses looked as if they had the edge. The Division had lost Pratt, who now rested in a hospital with a huge black eye, courtesy of "a slight fracture of the skull," sustained in the previous game. The clubs played pretty evenly though the entire contest. The Braves attacked through the air early, as Root, Pratt's replacement, took a 20-yard pass from Barnes and ran 40 more yards for the score, but Barnes's kick failed for the extra point. In the second quarter, the Papooses retaliated, with a pass that put them on the 8-yard line. A run produced six points and a successful extra point put the visitors ahead. That's the way the game ended, at least in scoring. In the third stanza, Barnes, about to be tackled, flipped the ball to Halme, who passed to Root, who sent a lateral to Barnes, who dispatched the oval to Root, who ran 55 yards to the frosh 8-yard line. But there the Papooses held, and without a consistent field-goal kicker, the Braves gave up the ball. The loss broke Norfolk's winning string at four and, according to the William & Mary paper, ruined the Division homecoming.[16]

The next contest supposedly would pit the Division against the Blue Imps, the undefeated freshmen of Duke University. Even though the Braves would likely lose such a contest—against players who would vie for a national title in a year or two—such a contest would give the Division program lots of prestige. But the contest at Foreman Field was cancelled because of heavy rain; the Division received a "hard blow" because of the cancellation.[17]

Anticlimactically, the season came to an end the weekend before Thanksgiving as the Norfolk eleven took on the Navy Base Boots, who came to Foreman Field along with their famous mascot, "Uncle Bill," an unusually craggy-looking goat. The base failed to bring its usual contingent of a thousand sailors, so only 700 chilled fans saw the game. Because the Boots had earlier beaten the William & Mary frosh and the Division had lost to the same team, a local reporter predicted a narrow win for the visitors. Despite negative predictions, the Braves won rather easily due to their strong team defense and an offense powerful enough to force the Boots back on their heels. On the first Norfolk drive, the Braves reached the Navy Boots' 7-yard line, where Halme missed a field-goal attempt. Halme's end runs and passes by Barnes kept up the pressure, but the Braves did not break into the scoring column until one-armed Jack Harris intercepted a pass around midfield. Halme then carried for a first down and Barnes passed to Louis Smith at the 15, and the end took it across the goal. Halme managed to kick for the extra point. After holding off a Boot threat, the Braves captured the ball at the enemy 40, and after a Barnes pass to Root moved the ball to the 13-yard line, Halme carried the oval four times for the final score of 13-0. The season ended with Norfolk achieving a record of 5-3, an improvement over the previous year, and one that kept the tradition of having decent seasons in odd-numbered years. Bill Pratt edged out Walter Halme in scoring points, 42-39.[18]

Although several players, including Woody Barnes, hung up their spikes after the 1937 season, fans had high hopes for 1938. Returning for a second year was John "Jack Rabbit" Brown, who was such a well-rounded athlete that he was considered Norfolk's answer to Jim Thorpe. New players like George Carroll, a one-time Maury High triple threat, Buddy Byers from Cradock High and a future professional player, and Benny Brock looked as if they had real potential in the backfield to go along with Captain Jack Harris, Johnny Edmonds and Walter Halme at fullback. Scott at first shifted a recovered Sid Krukin to end but then decided he might be successful at quarterback. A Harris twisted ankle seems to have necessitated that experiment. Guards George Harper and Jim Knighton, Vince Pezzella at center, Jimmy Gildner, Bill Turville and Monte Oden were to open up as the linemen. Big Bill Rodgers would return, after missing some of the previous season and the first two games of the current campaign. Other possibilities included Milton Mauck, an all-star from the Community League, Jimmy Sullivan, from one of the other recreational leagues, Albert Wescott, another Community High League all-star, Donald Joseph from Churchland, and Oscar Wergley, still another Community High League star. Eddie Tyler later received publicity when he had to have stitches to close a wound near his eye.[19]

With 45 men out for the team, the editor of the campus newspaper, expressing unbounded optimism, urged all students to take advantage of the student activity pass, which the students paid for whether or not they used it. Exuding an unusual degree of confidence about the potential for the 1938 team, the editor stated that those in the "know" thought the team "has the power, the reserve and the spirit to take the games scheduled." He apparently believed that the team had a good chance to go undefeated. The editor, urging the students to be enthusiastic supporters, looked forward to an "unprecedented crowd" for the game against the Naval Training Station.[20]

The Naval Training Station sent its band, several hundred sailors, and a team that had been practicing since mid-August (nothing was said about the goat). Before the usual handful of Division students, the early part of the game went well enough for Scott's youngsters. Jack Harris intercepted a pass on his own 33-yard line and carried the ball across midfield. Faced with a fourth down and short yardage, Halme backed up and gunned the ball to freshman halfback Benny Brock, who cut sharply to his right and tiptoed along the sidelines for a touchdown. In the second half, the Boots matched the touchdown, and like Norfolk, messed up on the extra point. Midway through the fourth quarter, the Sailors, stopped deep in their rival's territory by "a fighting mad Division line" (according to Fergusson), resorted to the rarely used device: the field goal. The Boots' captain, who had played for the University of Alabama, made good on the place kick, giving the visitors a 9-6 triumph.[21]

Playing at Richmond near the end of September, the Division sustained a second loss, 6-2, when the Spider quarterback picked up a loose ball and ran for 94 yards. The score was a matter of dispute because the play came as a result of a long, low Halme punt, during which a referee blew his whistle for a holding call. The quarterback, however, picked up the ball on the 6, sneaked up to midfield, and dashed for the goal. Assuming the play was dead, no Brave even tried to lay a hand on him. Norfolk scored on a blocked punt recovered by a Richmond player in his own end zone. Harris missed the game because he had injured his hand in a scrimmage and needed stitches. Everett Tolson and George Carroll both practiced at directing the offense, and Carroll got the assignment. So the situation now stood the way it had the previous year, with the team record at 0-2. The Braves hoped for the same thing that had happened in October in 1937—a winning streak.[22]

Harris recovered sufficiently to direct the attack in the next encounter, when the Braves, "passed and smashed their way" to an easy win over Hampden-Sydney's freshmen. Only a handful of fans watched "Blond Blizzard" Walter Halme score two touchdowns and make one of three extra-point attempts. George Carroll broke through for another touchdown and—wonder of wonders—John Brown cashed in a field goal at the beginning of the fourth quarter. Brown, a "slippery hipped youngster," according to Fergusson, also made some good runs. Cecil Griffin caught some passes, as did the other end, Sid Kruken. Lanky Everett Tolson broke away for some long gains late in the game. Although the victory came at the expense of one of the weaker elevens on the Brave schedule, Scott was undoubtedly happy that his club had broken into the win column.[23]

The hoped-for streak failed to materialize as the Division faced a much tougher foe in the next game—the freshmen from VMI. The Little Keydets were led by Nelson Catlett, a former great for Hampton High School. In practices before the contest, Scott tried out Mahlon Funk—who usually played end—in the backfield to help out Carroll, Halme and Brown. As expected, Catlett gave the Braves fits, as the "smooth-working, confident" Keydets rolled for two touchdowns while shutting out the Division, in every sense of the word. They even held the Division without a first down. The 14-0 score would have been much higher, but the stalwart Division defense, with soaring punts from Carroll and Halme, and two stands on the 1-yard line, kept the score respectable.[24]

Jack Harris, the great one-armed blocking back, returned to quarterback, doubtless along with high hopes that he could provide the impetus necessary to move the offense. The use of a system where the center hiked the ball directly to one of four men in the backfield allowed Scott to make Harris his principal signal-caller. The press favored the Braves against the next adversary, the Panthers of North Carolina's High Point College, but the visitors proved to have much bigger players than anticipated. Scott's men also missed many offensive assignments, especially when the Braves completed short passes. Early on, Lee Reppert, a little-used tackle, blocked a High Point kick on the 25, and Jim Knighton recovered the ball. Two end sweeps by Brown brought the ball to the 12, but an interception ended the threat. In the second quarter, the visitors mounted a long drive, which ended when a Panther runner trotted through a gaping hole in the Division defense for a touchdown. Desperation passes brought the Braves to midfield in the third quarter. A subsequent punt by Carroll put the visitors back on their own 6-yard line. On an ensuing drive, the Braves, according to Fergusson, "resorted to 'Old 83,'" but maybe it was "Old 88," if Brown's account is accurate. Whatever the number or direction, the screen pass to Harris produced a 23-yard gain, but the attack again bogged down and the game ended with Norfolk losing, 7-0.[25]

Georgetown University sent a talented freshman team, weighing on average 200 pounds, that expected to wallop the Braves. In 1941, many of these players would win 23 straight games as members of the varsity team and would even participate in the Orange Bowl. The home club hoped to stay in the game with its passing attack. The "Baby Hoyas" won, but only by scoring the lone touchdown of the contest late in the fourth period. The intrepid Braves stopped the freshmen five times inside the 15-yard marker. Cecil Griffin made a key interception, ending one of these threats. Forty-three years later, Griffin recalled that he was sitting on the bench when Scott sent him back into the game as the Hoyas threatened. He sacked a runner for a 10-yard loss and recovered a fumble to stop the threat. On another occasion, Carroll boomed a kick, according to long-time *Virginian-Pilot* reporter Abe Goldblatt, 90 yards "in the air" (John Brown says a very stiff wind was blowing), but the Braves later gave the visitors the ball on their 28. The visitors dominated the game, as was expected, making 14 first downs to but one for the home team, but Griffin thought it was "one of the finest moments for Norfolk Division football as well as myself." Once clocked in a 100-yard dash at 9.9 seconds compared to Brown's 9.8, Griffin was a star on the Division football and basketball teams, a natural athlete.[26]

Gutsy though the performance was, the Division had now lost five of its first six games. Worse still, Walter Halme, George Harper and Monte Oden sustained injuries and were expected either not to play or to play hurt in the next encounter, against the freshmen from William & Mary. Even though Scott considered using Jimmy Sullivan at end instead of Oden, on game day only Halme and Harper were missing from the starting lineup. Guard George Harper played some, even attempting a field goal from the 12-yard line, but the ball did not have sufficient height. After yielding a first-half touchdown to the visitors and playing generally listless ball in the early going, the Braves came alive in the second half. They scored on an 80-yard drive, primarily employing off-tackle thrusts, except when John Brown went around left end for 15 yards. Carroll then sneaked to the Papoose 10. After two plays netted little, Brown went around right end for the score. The visitors blocked Harris's attempt for an extra point. The game ended as a tie, even though the Braves drove deep into enemy terrain in the fourth quarter.

Big George Carroll had the longest run of the afternoon, for 26 yards, being overtaken and brought down by a lone defender on the 28. He also bulled his way to the 11, but the offense could get no further. The William & Mary paper claimed its men had played their best game of the season, scoring on an early drive but missing on a wide kick. The paper maintained that the frosh "completely outplayed their rivals during the first half," with only George Carroll's punting keeping down the score. And so, the "Papoose squad spoiled an otherwise perfect Homecoming for their brothers from Norfolk Division," but at least it was not a loss.[27]

the Division won its second game of the season in a game it dominated against East Carolina Teachers College on Armistice Day. Played at Foreman Field, the Teachers held off four Brave attacks after Mahlon Funk's touchdown run, 6-0 in the first quarter. Paul Bacalis, George Harper, Jack Harris, George Carroll and Funk all excelled during the contest.[28]

During the last game, this one against Wingate College from North Carolina, Scott had his hand above his eyes, either in deep thought or from what the press described as "coaching misery." But the defense did well, and the offense, buoyed by a 45-yard pass from George Carroll to Cecil Griffin, brought the ball to the 20. Mahlon Funk carried the ball several times, and finally took it over the goal for one of the few scores for the season. Monte Oden scored the extra point—the only one that year—on a Carroll pass. The season's record stood at 3 wins, 5 losses, and 1 tie, the worst ever experienced by a Brave eleven to that point. But with high school games now taken out of the equation, it could have been expected, despite the student paper's pre-season optimism.[28]

This 1936 Braves team finished the year with a 4–4 record. Pictured from left to right are (front row) Douglas Gildner, Woody Barnes, Lowery, McDonald Chapman, Maury Riganto, Johnny Doyle, Ernest Vance, Henry Miles, Gifford James Dodson; (middle row) Bagley, Preston Matthews, Billy Miller, Carter, Jennings, John Spencer, Claiborne Nixon, James Padgett, Buchanan, Edwin Barsell; (back row) Henson, Adams, Sidney Krukin, Raymond Baldwin, Stell, Macon, Fred Edmonds, Jiminez, Joynes, Davis, and Manager Cason. (Courtesy of Special Collections and University Archives, Perry Library, Old Dominion University)

From 1936 to 1938, Sidney "Sid" Alexander Krukin played left end for Norfolk Division. A graduate of Maury High School, Krukin also played basketball for the Braves under Coach Tommy Scott. (Courtesy of Sargeant Memorial Room, Norfolk Public Library)

Johnny "Jack Rabbit" Brown held a stronghold on the tailback position in Tommy Scott's backfields from 1936 to 1939. Brown was such a well-rounded athlete that he was considered Norfolk's answer to Jim Thorpe. Besides football, he was a star for the Division in baseball and track and field. Later, Brown would become an exceptional coach and administrator for Norfolk's Granby High School. (Courtesy of Sargeant Memorial Room, Norfolk Public Library)

At the age of nine, Jack Harris lost his right arm while jumping a freight train in Norfolk's Lambert Point. This did not deter Harris, as he became a three-sport star at the former Oceana High School in Princess Anne County (Virginia Beach). When he arrived at the Norfolk Division, he decided to concentrate on football and baseball. He served as a halfback and quarterback for Tommy Scott from 1937 to 1938. Earning the nickname "One-Armed Brave," he led the team in interceptions during his time at the Division. His career was just as impressive on the baseball field, as he also led the squad from the mound. Completing his education at Columbia University, he would return to Norfolk and become a sports announcer and later a radio executive. (Courtesy of Sargeant Memorial Room, Norfolk Public Library)

This 1937 photograph, with the stands of Foreman Field in the background, show Norfolk Division ends Louis Guy and Louis "Hickey" Smith. This would be Guy's only year with the team while Smith had also played the previous year. (Courtesy of Sargeant Memorial Room, Norfolk Public Library)

George Carroll poses in a passing position for the camera in this wonderful photograph. A triple-threat player for Maury High, Carroll would handle quarterback duties for the Braves from 1937 to 1938. (Courtesy of Sargeant Memorial Room, Norfolk Public Library)

In 1937 Walter Halme, the great Maury player of its 1935 state championship team, transferred to the Norfolk Division from Duke University. His performance for the freshman team at Duke had earned him a comparison to the school's All-American and Portsmouth native, Ace Parker. While at the Division, this handsome blond-headed youngster, nicknamed "Swede," left his impact for the Braves with his long runs, touchdowns, and field-goal kicking. After his career with the Division, Halme would play for the Norfolk Shamrocks, the city's entry in the Dixie League. (Courtesy of Sargeant Memorial Room, Norfolk Public Library)

A Naval Base defender attempts to knock the ball down before it reaches a Brave's outstretched arms. For three quarters the game would be nip-and-tuck, but midway in the fourth quarter a field goal by the Boots captain, a former University of Alabama player, secured the team a 9-6 victory. (Courtesy of Sargeant Memorial Room, Norfolk Public Library)

Tommy Scott sits during the last game of the 1938 season against Wingate College, either in deep thought or in what the press described in the morning paper as "coaching misery." Although the Braves won the game, it was only their third win for the season. (Courtesy of Sargeant Memorial Room, Norfolk Public Library)

A Virginian-Pilot *reporter referred to these players as "grim-looking individuals" as they prepare for a 1938 game against High Point College. From left to right are backs Buddy Byers, Donald Joseph and Oscar Wegley, and center Paul Bacalis.* (Courtesy of Sargeant Memorial Room, Norfolk Public Library)

Posing for this 1938 photograph before an upcoming game with Hampden-Sydney are from left to right, linemen Bill Turville, Jim Knighton, Eddie Tyler and Hugh Sykes. (Courtesy of Sargeant Memorial Room, Norfolk Public Library)

In 1939, playing their first year of varsity football at the Norfolk Division are Cecil Griffin (left) and Jimmy Sullivan (right). (Courtesy of Sargeant Memorial Room, Norfolk Public Library)

Posing for this 1938 photograph before an upcoming game with Hampden-Sydney, are from left to right, linemen Bill Turville, Jim Knighton, Eddie Tyler and Hugh Sykes. (Courtesy of Sargeant Memorial Room, Norfolk Public Library)

CHAPTER SIX

Final Years of Football in a More Threatening World, 1939–1940

In September 1939, most of Europe went to war, an act that soon put many young men who played for the Norfolk Division on the road to military service. The editor of the campus newspaper took the occasion of the Division's first football game to observe that, unlike much of the world, "our boys are fighting, perhaps through mud and slime but without trenches and barbed wire." He hoped that would always be the case.[1]

As usual, pre-season commentators predicted a successful year, enamored with the mix of veterans and newcomers on the squad, even though Scott had no idea who would do most of the kicking or passing. For just the second time in school history, Scott had to make a cut to reduce the number of players to a manageable 40. Tom Fergusson figured Scott was "well fortified with reserve strength" and had a "wealth of backs," so one could certainly expect more offensive output.[2]

Bernie Shapiro, a former Maury man who already had experience at the University of Georgia, brought some weight and experience to the guard position. Elwood Warren, a former star at Wilson High, held down a tackle slot. More interested in playing football than studying, Bill Baker, another Wilson man who had played for the VMI freshmen the previous year, rode with Warren from Portsmouth every day in an old Austin, crossing over the Elizabeth River on the ferry. He looked good in the line as a reserve.[3]

Paul Bacalis and Vince Pezella had experience at center. Newcomer Al Kaufman, weighing 195 pounds, would surely help out in the line. Big Morton McCarthy, one of Tidewater's finest golfers, would make a fine tackle. Dorsey Cooper, a pitcher for the Division baseball squad, could play either tackle or end. Among the other possible ends was John Peterson, a Maury backup player the year before but who had added some 20 pounds over the year. Jimmy Cole and Joe Scherberger looked good as reserves. Bob Kinnard, out of Georgia, also looked capable. Jimmy Macon, Jack Dee, Cecil Griffin, George Wilbur, Pat McCarthy and Harold Hudgins, a star for Maury the previous year, all looked like prospective linemen. Mahlon Funk and Joe Brichter, both holdovers from the previous year, were injured in the early practices, but were expected to be mainstays once the season officially started. The likely starting backfield included speedy John Brown at halfback, Fred Nardini (a star from Connecticut) at halfback, Carl Hull (from the Community League) at fullback and Jack Moore (who had played well for the William & Mary frosh against the Division the previous year) at quarterback. Early in the season, however, Moore damaged the cartilage in his knee, thereby jeopardizing his playing time. Backup blocking backs included Everett Tolson, who also might have possibilities as a passer, Benny Brock, Buddy Byers, Gus Carnezis, Bill Dunn, and Joe Hatfield from Kempsville. Overall, the Division had plenty of players from which the right combination might emerge. However, according to Baker, several on the team would never see any game action.

Once again, the season started with a loss, as the Little Spiders of Richmond passed for two scores in the fourth quarter. The Braves outplayed the visitors for three-fourths of the game, but gave way under the heat and the suddenly lively Spider offense. Moore came close to scoring on a long punt return, but went down at the 9-yard line when a defender grabbed his ankle from behind.[5]

During an easy 27-0 triumph in early October, Ray Sutton, an All-League selection in the Community League in 1937, romped 56 yards for the game's last touchdown against an Apprentice eleven out of the Norfolk Navy Yard. Sutton also scored on a 2-yard plunge.

Carl Hull's interception in the second quarter indirectly led to the second score. Substitute guard Bill Baker intercepted a pass and ran 50 yards for a touchdown.

But the Division lost its next game, 7-0, to High Point College, when the Panthers drove the ball over the chalk line in the second quarter, and the Division stalled at the 1-foot line on the last play of the game. Scant coverage of the game reveals only that Norfolk played more or less its regular lineup in the game in North Carolina.[6]

The Baby Hoyas of Georgetown routed the Braves in Washington, D.C. The visitors stood up well for three quarters, trailing only 12-6 going into the final stanza. They had scored after Fred Nardini intercepted a pass on his 29-yard line. Joe Britcher connected on several passes, the last one "grooved" to John Peterson on the Georgetown 7-yard line. The Brave end dragged a would-be tackler into the end zone for Norfolk's only score of the game. In the fourth quarter, the home team broke through for 27 points and a 39-6 rout.[7]

The Braves, however, got back on the winning track by outplaying East Carolina at Greenville. The visitors went into the game with a lengthy injury list, mostly incurred playing against Georgetown. It supposedly included Paul Bacalis at end, Jack Moore, Bob Kinnard and Bernie Shapiro (now considered a tackle). Holding their rivals to but three first downs, the visitors dominated play on both offense and defense, but their only touchdown came when Johnny Brown picked up a bouncing ball on his own 15 and scurried for 85 (75 by one account) yards for the score. Johnny can't recall the exact number of yards, but does remember Bacalis giving him a huge hug after the score. He also recalls the sand burrs that made playing on the field in Greenville unpleasant. Bill Baker placed the extra point through the uprights to produce a 7-0 win. Baker, the future mayor of Portsmouth, recalled the same sand burrs but also the girls, who far outnumbered the boys at the Teachers College campus. Upon meeting the Division bus, one co-ed yelled, "Fresh Meat!"[8]

The now traditional game against the Naval Training Station surprisingly proved to be a relatively easy 13-0 win, as the Division went one up on its record in the first weekend of November. The Braves, according to Fergusson, emitted "a full-throated war cry" and a potent aerial attack as Johnny Brown, Everett Tolson, John Peterson and Joe Brichter led the way. Substitute tackle Richard Scherberger also scored for the winners.[9]

The day before Armistice Day, the Braves, according to Joe Leslie, writing for the school newspaper, "hung up another scalp," as the Division triumphed over Newport News

Apprentice (probably only its first-year men). No one scored for the first three quarters, and then Joe Brichter hit Johnny Peterson on a fourth-down pass, putting the ball on the Apprentice 16, whereupon Peterson scampered into the end zone. On the next Norfolk series, Brown swept right end for another score. Shortly thereafter, Peterson made a beautiful reception, this one on a pass from Everett Tolson near the Builder 25. Then Brichter drove for a 24-yard gain to the defenders' 1-yard line, where Tolson passed to Carl Hull for the last six points. In the 12-minute quarter, the Braves amassed 26 points, likely the greatest number of points ever scored by the Division in such a brief time.[10]

A confident Division eleven now took on the powerful North Carolina State freshmen, but that confidence was severely shaken when the visitors scored nine points in the first quarter. Center Paul Bacalis hiked the ball over Brichter's head into the end zone, where the punter fell on it for a safety. On the ensuing kickoff, the Baby Wolves lucked out when they recovered their own fumble, allowing them to drive forward for a touchdown and an extra point. The Division defense then stiffened, as both clubs traded interceptions several times. Early in the second half, the Brave aerial assault finally bore fruit, as Peterson took a "Slats" Tolson pass for 26 yards, followed by another Tolson pass to Johnny Brown for another 26. With the ball on the enemy 20, Tolson backed up and zipped a pass down the middle to Peterson, who, catching it on the 2, fell into the end zone. Although the visitors blocked the extra-point attempt, the Division seemed to be back in the game, particularly when they secured the ball again. But an interception and a subsequent score by the Wolves put them beyond reach, even though their attempted drop-kick for an extra point failed. The 15-6 loss to a powerful adversary was nothing to be ashamed of, but it ended a three-game winning streak, and meant that their next game against the William & Mary freshmen would determine whether the Braves could sustain the tradition of having winning seasons in odd-numbered years.[11]

Although William & Mary's Papooses were favored, being heavier and more versatile, the Braves pulled ahead in the first half, 13-0, before some 1,500 paying customers and 500 school children who were admitted for free to help fill up spacious Foreman Field. In the beginning of the game, Everett Tolson, according to Fergusson, resembled a professional as he "pitched passes," with Peterson usually on the receiving end. Also, Johnny Brown made a "miraculous" catch on the 7 and then carried it to the 3, where on the next play, he ran into the end zone. Paul Bacalis then placed one through the uprights for the extra point.

In the second quarter, Jimmy Macon, substituting for Kinnard, recovered a fumble on the Papoose 33-yard line. A cross-field pass found Peterson "racing at breakneck speed toward the south end of the field." At the last second, reaching up, he speared the oval in a "sleight-of-hand" maneuver, followed by a short run for the score. At some point late in the first half, a William & Mary player put an elbow directly onto Brown's head, giving him a concussion. He awoke in the hospital, where Tommy Scott told him the team had lost.[12]

Presumably the William & Mary coach gave a stirring pep talk at halftime because the freshmen came roaring back with three touchdowns and held the Braves scoreless, as the game and season came to an end for the home team. The William & Mary paper attributed the poor frosh showing in the first half to overconfidence and generally criticized what was supposed to be a nucleus to carry William & Mary, under varsity coach Carl Voyles, into national greatness. Even though the Papooses had outscored opponents 125-39 during the season, they had narrowly lost to the Richmond freshmen and the narrow margin of victory over the Division could hardly be ignored. The writer also implied some concern about the academic qualifications of some of the players. This loss meant that the Division ended up with an overall record of four wins, six losses, and two ties in contests against the freshmen of the parent school. This game ended the series, even though the Division fielded a team the next year. The season's record was a disappointing 4-5.[13]

In February 1940, the campus newspaper expressed some serious doubt about whether intercollegiate football would continue, as students talked about emphasizing intramural sports rather than the more costly competitive variety. Moving in the opposite direction, Scott and Director Walter Hodges worked on upgrading the schedule and the quality of players. Hodges wrote to Voyles about sending football players who could not meet entrance requirements at the parent college to the Division. The Division, according to Hodges, could accept high school graduates that had not taken an academic program. Apparently Voyles had already communicated with Hodges about the idea, because the Division director contended that Voyles was the only one in Williamsburg who saw the "farm possibilities" at the Division.

In 1940, the Division decided it would no longer play freshmen teams or junior colleges. Around the same time, Scott's correspondence indicates that he was concerned about competing for high school players who had been ballyhooed in the press. Unable to obligate the school for four-year scholarships, he wanted to recruit lesser-known high school players for work study and later transfer them to regular scholarships. Any aid for athletes was a contentious issue at the time, but the practice was fairly common. A year or so earlier, for example, Scott had arranged for Bill Pratt to receive a National Youth Administration grant. When Joe Britcher transferred to campus from Centre College well after the start of the 1938 fall semester, Hodges found a scholarship for him, probably financed by local businessmen. Hodges also promised Bill Baker, he "would be taken care of."[14]

Employing these tactics would certainly indicate a coming of age for the Norfolk Division, but Hodges and Scott wanted to suspend football for a season to gear up for the new status. As columnist Cox described the change in a letter to the coach at Guilford College, the Division was "looking ahead to a time in the near future when they will be a full four-year school." No matter the number of losses and only having freshmen and sophomores, "they will operate their athletics on a regular college basis."

Cox continued that among their assets was a "splendid athletic plant, including the best football stadium in the state." To transition into the new plan, those in charge of athletics (Scott and Hodges) had "decided to forsake football for next fall," but, Cox added: "I, for one, encouraged them to keep on playing at any cost." This explains why he hoped Guilford would consider scheduling games with the Division.[15]

By the time the 1940 season rolled around, the federal government had imposed a military draft, despite which enrollment at the Division remained around 500, largely because the original draft age of eligibility was 21, not 18, as it later became. Only 12 students showed up for the first football practice, forcing Scott to comb the campus for more players. Abe Goldblatt claimed that coach Scott faced similar situations in the past, suggesting that somehow Scott would find a way to field a successful eleven. As expected, many youngsters moved on, Johnny Peterson finding a place on the roster of the parent institution. The situation seemed dire, especially when Scott had to be hospitalized for several days because of a throat problem. But there was some talent. An experienced Ray Sutton mastered the drop kick, big lefty John Upton looked as if he could hold down punting assignments, and Fred Nardini and Jimmy Macon looked like a good pass combination. Captain Bernie Shapiro, who had played the previous year, would play center instead of tackle. Either Clarence Tynes, who played a little the previous year, or Mike Traetto, out of New Jersey, might be able to replace the bigger Morton McCarthy. Sam Hopkins, Dick Scherberger, and "Big Jim" Rodgers might be helpful. In time, more players joined up, but others left, a standard scenario during the program's entire existence.[16]

With a tough schedule, reduced personnel, and an ailing coach, the Division experienced its worst season ever. The powerful High Point College Panthers rolled over the Division, 33-0, at Foreman Field to start the season. A young and inexperienced East Carolina Teachers College had little trouble in disposing of the Braves in a Friday afternoon affair, 18-0. Former assistant coach Buck Miles helped out some, but the team really had no coach, compelling Tom Fergusson to describe the condition of the club's performance against the Trojans as akin to a "rudderless ship at sea."[17]

With Scott not able to continue full-time coaching, the Division turned to George Stirnweiss for assistance. He had played baseball in the Piedmont League for the Norfolk Tars the previous summer and was now playing football for the Dixie League's Shamrocks, a team that Scott had started the season coaching, along with his numerous duties at the Division. Known as the "Flying Dutchman," Stirnweiss had starred in several sports for the University of North Carolina. Later known as "Snuffy," he would lead the American League in hitting in 1945 while playing for the New York Yankees (his .309 average is among the lowest ever for a batting champion). A physical education major, he planned to finish undergraduate work the next spring and move on for a master's degree. Although he knew a thing or two about football, there was little he could do to turn the tide for the Braves. The losses continued.[18]

Undefeated Belmont Abbey, out of the Tar Heel State, came to town. Although their eleven had little heft, the Crusaders were fast and experienced and had not been beaten in several campaigns. They had even less trouble than the other two visitors, rolling to a 48-0 victory.

The Apprentice club, over which Scott's men had little trouble winning the previous year, proved nearly invincible, as the Builders scored touchdowns in the first, second, and fourth quarters in a 21-0 triumph. The Division managed to make seven first downs, but its offense seemingly failed to come near the shadows of the other team's goal posts.

Sutton's 71-yard run on a short pass from Nardini, to the opponent's 14 seemed to be the high point of the season, but Jimmy Macon and Johnnie Upton also deserved praise.[19]

In the wake of the loss to Apprentice, the campus press took notice of the Division's state of affairs. One student wrote there must be "something haywire somewhere," when a team always loses by "lopsided margins." In the belief that the material existed for a good team, he placed the blame largely on the student body, which he thought had "no spirit, no pep, no life." In trying to rally the students behind the team, he urged creating a real cheerleading squad and having more bonfires. In addition, he said his fraternity was willing to hold more dances to raise money to replace the old uniforms, pads in poor shape and shoes that did not fit. Another writer confirmed the condition of the equipment, but took some space to praise the effort in holding down Apprentice (noting especially that the students who attended actually made some noise and that more faculty came in support than were usually seen).[20]

the Division then played against Bergen College. Already shorthanded, the Braves faced the strong northern New Jersey eleven with several players either out of the game (Tynes, Shapiro and center West) or, like Scherberger, nursing injuries. Johnny Blackwell had to plug up one of the guard slots, while Jim Rodgers and Sam Hopkins held down the tackle positions. Fred Nardini, Jonny Upton and Roy Sutton comprised three-fourths of the backfield, but George French, Dick Hoskin and Max Wilcox would either start or play quite a bit against the invaders. On the eve of another loss, columnist Cox watched the "handful of boys" practice as a cold wind swept across the stadium field. "Over-matched, beset by injuries and ignored," the "new men in strange positions" struggled on.

The columnist pointed out that the Division had formally given up football the previous winter, but at the urgings of Scott and the players (he failed to mention his role in the affair), the institution let them carry on without college help. Exactly what Cox meant by this remark is unclear, but he urged the members of the community not necessarily to go to the game, but at least to think about the players at game time, and honor those who "refuse to be whipped."[21]

Another 21-0 loss marked the occasion for the Braves, the Division only advancing near the enemy 30-yard line. Only 26 paying customers at 50 cents each attended the last game ever played in Foreman Field by the Norfolk Division. Seventy-four others paid 5 cents each for passes and 546 students had free access but most did not come. Revenue from tickets ran a grand total of $16.70. When concessions, programs and whatever else might pass for income came in, the Division took in almost $23, and thus only absorbed a loss of $6, not counting whatever was promised to Bergen College for making the trip.[22]

With little fanfare and almost no news coverage, the Braves went on the road for the first time that season—to face Bluefield College in West Virginia. The game ended predictably with the home team victorious, 25-0. The Division lost all its six games that season, and also came nowhere near even *threatening* to score.[23]

Just after the season ended and facing stomach surgery and another hospital stay, Scott resigned. Director Hodges accepted the decision with regret. Despite his youth, Scott's length of service to the college was exceeded by only one other member of the faculty. Scott came through the operation fine, but one of the reporters also noted that no one had responded to the want ad for Scott's replacement. While this possibly reflected the improving employment picture, mostly, according to the newsman, it was due to the job's excessive demands and low pay.[24]

With Scott no longer on the staff, the Division brought on Sam Kamen, a former star athlete with the parent institution, to help coach and carry out duties as physical education teacher, along with Joe "Scrap" Chandler. After coaching basketball in the winter and spring football practice, Stirnweiss would return to playing professional baseball. Doubtless thinking about the problems with 1940 football and the lack of baseball that same year, Bill Rosenfeld, the graduate manager, expressed the opinion that "things will be different" the next year. They certainly were, but not in the way Rosenfeld expected.[25]

Sometime after accepting Scott's resignation, Hodges himself was forced to vacate the directorship of the college after it was discovered that he had altered the coursework of 38 students. Whether football players received any special help is not known because names of students rightly remained anonymous. Based on these charges, the president of the College of William & Mary demanded Hodges's removal. An almost unanimous outcry rose out of the usually subdued student body and among city leaders. In the end, the parent institution let Hodges stay, but only as director of adult education. Soon thereafter, he left the Division to become the director of the Civilian Defense Program for Hampton Roads.

At the first spring football practice ever held in the school's history, Kamen and

Stirnweiss assessed the available talent. Among the players were John Upton, Fred Nardini, Clarence Tynes, Mike Traetto, Sam Hopkins, Hewitt Dunn (once all-state at Maury), Bob Faherty, Harold Treakle (another end and Maury man) and Tom Ward. It looked like a solid nucleus to go against the same colleges that had been played the previous year, plus Guilford and Davis-Elkins, even with more than half the games on the road. There were even plans to have rallies and organized cheerleading, two fringe benefits that the teams had been doing without for the program's entire existence.[26]

In the summer, however, the Division dropped football. This decision resulted not from mobilization of the national defense, including a military draft, fudging of student records, or even finicky finances. The Division's new director, Charles Duke, claimed he was forced to withdraw from contracts with several schools with which the Division had scheduled games. In asking to be let out of the contracts he explained that the Southern Conference demanded that the Division either stop playing sophomores and freshmen on the same teams or sever connections with the two members of the conference: William & Mary and Virginia Tech. In those times, and for many years thereafter, four-year colleges could not play freshmen with upper classmen. Because the Division was part of the two institutions of higher education, the conference applied the rule to the Norfolk Division, even though only a few of its students took classes for more than two years. In giving the reasons to the press, Duke also noted that football "had not paid its way at the Division for years."[27]

Although the campus paper pretty much concurred with Duke that the Southern Conference was to blame for terminating football at the Division, columnist Bill Cox presented a somewhat different interpretation about the demise of Division football. Despite spring training, Cox thought the end had been "forecast for some time by the grid doctors." But "Stirney put on a spring practice, talked football to beat the band and kindled a few fires." Young men loved the game, an assertion proved the previous season by the conduct of the Braves, "who pulled together to the end of an all-losing season." Cox, unlike Duke, explained the termination of the sport on the inability to arrange a good schedule, known football powers not wanting to take a chance of losing to the school. With a weak schedule, "their own students refuse to back them, much less Mr. Public."

Further complicating the issue was the concern of some Southern Conference teams that William & Mary would "use the Division as a sort of football farm." Such was not the case, but the conference, which controlled eligibility issues "in this part of the country" failed to understand the status of the Division. In his requiem for the program, Cox never explained how he thought a junior college was supposed to compete against full-fledged colleges. It is possible that he and Hodges assumed the Division would soon be a four-year college. That assumption prevailed before World War II, but the school did not attain that status until the mid-1950s.[28]

Reading between the lines, it seems as if Duke was all too willing to concede the matter of the Division's status. It would be hard to imagine Hodges giving in so readily to what looks like a flawed understanding about the connection between a branch and a tree in higher education. Why Southern Conference officials would think a junior college, with connections to two well-known colleges, should have to abide by the same rules as the parent institutions defies comprehension. Also, one wonders why the same policy did not apply to basketball and other sports in which the Division participated. No matter the real reason for ending the program, it would have been nearly impossible to continue to play football with the loss of so many males in the student body due to the war.

With the need for any new WPA projects diminishing in 1941, the city of Norfolk still managed to get more than its share of federal funds under the Federal Works Agency, created under the Lanham Act, which was designed to give aid specifically for educational purposes in areas affected by the defense buildup. As a result of that act, the Norfolk Division campus acquired new dressing rooms added to the rear of the federally funded classroom building immediately adjacent to Foreman Field. Additionally, the space under Foreman Field's east-side stands was converted for use in various defense-related instruction, such as work on motors.[29]

Thanks to a wide variety of sources, we have quite a bit of information on those who played football for the Division and served their nation in World War II. The war dead included Adrian Dorsey Cooper Jr., Herbert C. Moore, Albert Kaufmann, Carl T. Hull Jr., Richard R. James, Wilson "Dick" Dozier and David A. "Pete" Dozier.

Pete Dozier, who enlisted in the Army Air Force at Langley in January 1942, served in the Caribbean against German "wolf packs" and was deemed missing in action while stationed in the Panama Canal Zone in late 1944. Captured by the Japanese as a result of a bombing run over Kobe, Japan, there is reason to believe that Hull was beheaded along with others in his crew as a war criminal, certainly not a typical method of treating prisoners of war. Albert Kauffmann died while training as a pilot, and Dick James, another pilot, failed to survive a steep dive. Obviously those in the nation's air forces had a comparatively high exposure during the war, but one wonders why so many Division men signed up for such service.

Dick Dozier received his pilot training with the Royal Canadian Air Force, winning his wings at their training center in March of 1941. On the occasion of this achievement, he wrote a lengthy piece for the local press, describing the mental stamina needed to pass the solo tests. Using what is obviously a bit of literary license, he described the need for a hotel room, a girl and two cases of beer to "sort of unburden" oneself. During the war, he became a lieutenant in the U.S. Navy and served in the Pacific Theater with valor (earning a Purple Heart and Distinguished Flying Cross). According to former U.S. Congressman and long-time ODU teacher and administrator Bill Whitehurst, Dick was flying his tenth mission in the last phase of the Pacific War off the new *USS Yorktown*, when his F-6 Hellcat was shot down in an attack on a Japanese airfield on Honshu (a secondary target when the main one was engulfed by fog) in the southern part of Tokyo Bay on August 13, 1945, two days before the Japanese surrender. (Whitehurst flew as a radioman-machine gunner with the Torpedo Squadron of the same flying group, which was directed to a different target that day.)[30]

Of the numerous servicemen of the "Greatest Generation" who survived the war, Division men served in every branch of the military and in most theaters of action. Dick Scherberger led a platoon in an engineering combat battalion as American forces advanced through Europe. His brother, Joe, piloted Army planes on the Burma run. Bill Baker flew a B-29 with special radar designed to locate Japanese fuel depots and John Brown commanded tanks that, among other things, crossed the Rhine on a pontoon bridge. Cecil Griffin served in the Navy's V-7 program and after becoming an ensign at Columbia University, served on a minesweeper at Anzio. After the war, he commanded a U.S. Supply Depot in the Philippines.

Joe Brichter landed at Normandy a few days after D-Day and fought his way through the hedgerows of France. After directing traffic for the "Red Ball Express" and driving a jeep, he, along with the rest of General George Patton's division, was fighting his way into Germany around Thanksgiving 1944, when he was wounded.[31]

Despite the variety of military service, many from the Division gravitated toward serving on planes. Paul Bacalis, who had received pilot instruction at the Division, soon became a second lieutenant with a flying group stationed at Langley. Ensign James Cooper, who played three sports at the Division, had already received training and was serving as a naval inspector at the Naval Air Station at Pensacola nine months before Pearl Harbor.[32]

The 1939 Braves from left to right are (first row) Cole, McCarthy, Peterson, Dee, Bacalis, Shapiro, Hudgins, Hull, Baker, Tolson, Funk, (second row) Brown, J. Moore, Pezzella, H. Moore, J. Sherberger, Jones, Dunn, Karnezis, Dryden, Byers, (third row) Nordini, Macon, Ferguson, Tynes, Brichter, Griffin, Hatfield, Sutton, Brock, (fourth row) Hassell, Harshman, Cooper, Warren, Kaufman, R. Sherberger, Pyles, Blackwell, Reinburg, (back row) Wilber, Bisschop, Head Coach Tommy Scott, James, Trainer Jones, Reveille, Carlisle, and Dozier. (Courtesy of Sargeant Memorial Room, Norfolk Public Library)

A star for his New Haven, Connecticut, high school, Fred Nardini played halfback and quarterback the last two years that the Division fielded a team. (Courtesy of Sargeant Memorial Room, Norfolk Public Library)

In their first game of 1939, Division players watch from the sideline as the Braves take on the Baby Spiders. The Braves outplayed the visitors for three quarters, but gave way under the heat as the University of Richmond scored two touchdowns in the final quarter. (Courtesy of Sargeant Memorial Room, Norfolk Public Library)

Quarterback Jack Moore comes close to scoring on a long punt return, but is taken down on the 9-yard line as a Richmond player runs him down from behind. (Courtesy of Sargeant Memorial Room, Norfolk Public Library)

Johnny "Jack Rabbit" Brown regularly thrilled Braves spectators with his speed and leaping ability as evident in this game against Richmond. (Courtesy of Sargeant Memorial Room, Norfolk Public Library)

With Scott unable to coach full-time, the Division turned to George Stirnweiss (far right). A star at the University of North Carolina in several sports, he also played baseball for the Norfolk Tars. He held spring practice in 1941, but football was discontinued before any games were played. (Courtesy of Sargeant Memorial Room, Norfolk Public Library)

This is a view of Foreman Field, circa 1940. (Courtesy of Special Collections and University Archives, Perry Library, Old Dominion University)

1940 Braves starters, before their game against Bergen College. Standing are (left to right) John Upton, Dick Hoskins, Fred Nardini and Roy Sutton. Kneeling (left to right) are Dick Sherberger, Sam Hopkins, John Blackwell, Clarence Tynes, Mike Traetto and Max Wilcox. (Courtesy of Sargeant Memorial Room, Norfolk Public Library)

This photograph shows the Braves and Bergen College, playing the last game at Foreman Field. The Braves would lose the game, 21-0. Only 26 paying customers at 50 cents each attended. Seventy-four others paid 5 cents each for passes and 546 students had free access, but most did not come. Revenue from tickets ran a grand total of $16.70. Although the team would yet travel to Bluefield College, this game ended football at Foreman Field for the Norfolk Division. (Courtesy of Sargeant Memorial Room, Norfolk Public Library)

CHAPTER SEVEN

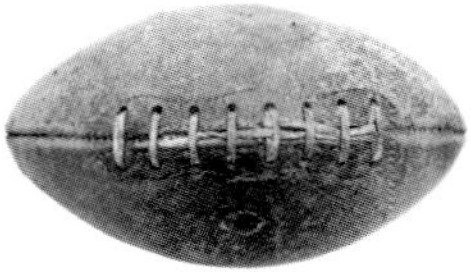

Football at Foreman Field Through the Years

With the loss to Bluefield, the curtain came down on football for the Division, but not for the campus. Any student who wanted to could easily take advantage of games at Foreman Field over the next 55 years. The number of games and quality of opponents, however, varied from year to year.

On New Year's Day 1941, Foreman Field became the site of Norfolk's first "bowl" game, when a team composed of recent college graduates and professionals took on a similar group from Richmond. Norfolk won the first "Smoke Bowl," 16-2, played before 5,000 with the net receipts going to benefit the Firemen's Mutual Aid Association, thus explaining the name of the contest. It turned out to be Norfolk's only experience with this particular bowl because after a return match in Richmond 11 months later, won by the capital city before about the same number of spectators, the series was not renewed. During that second game, Ace Parker (the famous athlete from Woodrow Wilson High School and Duke University) sustained a serious injury, despite which he returned to the National Football League. Reporter Tom Fergusson later claimed the first "Smoke Bowl" took place at night in 1940 in a game lost by William & Mary to NC State at Foreman

Field. It was called such because a heavy fog and smoke from a fire in the Dismal Swamp obscured proceedings.[1]

In its first year without any games of the Norfolk Division (1941), Foreman Field hosted high school games. Featuring Maury and Granby, they usually attracted around 4,000, although Granby, undefeated in its second football season, blanked Maury before 8,500, a pretty fair attendance since the game was not played on Thanksgiving.

In 1941, the most unique attraction turned out to be a rugby match between the crews of the *HMS Illustrious* and the *HMS Formidable*. The crew of the latter ship triumphed, 11-0, in rugby and 2-0 in the soccer game that preceded the rugby match. Ten thousand pro-British fans turned out for the occasion, with receipts derived from adult tickets going for 50 cents and military and children's for half that amount. The net income went to several cities in Great Britain recently damaged by German bombs during the "Battle for Britain." Reporters thought this was the first organized rugby match contested in Norfolk. Columnist Bill Cox, noting that experts thought American football grew out of English rugby, urged folks to attend the game and afterward jokingly (one hopes) suggested that the introduction of the forward pass would substantially improve the English game.[2]

The Shamrocks, coached by Stirnweiss and also led by Willard "Bolo" Perdue (of Duke University) and John Zontini (who played Minor League ball for the Portsmouth Cubs), moved their games to Foreman Field in 1941. A game scheduled in September that was to feature as referee the greatest American athlete of the first half of the 20th century, Jim Thorpe, was postponed when Zontini's father died as did the infant daughter of Portsmouth Cubs Coach Larry Weldon. The game was rescheduled for Sunday and thereby became the first professional football game ever played at Foreman Field on the Sabbath, drawing 7,500 fans.

With attendance ranging around 6,000, the Shamrocks went on to win the Dixie League title for the first time since 1938. The Shamrocks also won a mid-December encounter against Fort Story, supposedly the best military eleven around, in an effort to raise money for the Joy Fund, but only 1,500–"the smallest crowd of the season"–attended.[3]

Norfolk was fortunate that year to host two collegiate games. In one, the University of Virginia, featuring All-American Bill "Bluefield Bullet" Dudley, routed Virginia Tech before 15,000. In an earlier match-up, William & Mary easily conquered the George

Washington Colonials, 48-0, before half that number. Thus football fans in Norfolk got a chance to see Virginia, which had lost only to Yale of the Ivy League, and improving William & Mary, which had lost only two games, one to the Naval Academy and its last game of the season to North Carolina State.

One might think that World War II would be the death knell for collegiate sports at Foreman Field, but although some schools such as VPI gave up football for part of the war, others fielded teams for the entire era. In mid-November 1942, almost a year after American entrance into the war, undefeated William & Mary, with the best defensive team in the nation, overcame the "Flying Squadron" of the Keydets of VMI, 27-6, before 17,500 spectators. Earlier in November, Tech bested Virginia before a slim crowd of 6,000, a number more in keeping with a national trend that saw a 25-percent drop in collegiate football attendance.

Later that season, the Indians suffered their only loss, to the University of North Carolina Pre-flight School in a game not played at Foreman Field. Most of the institutions of higher learning that kept football did so because branches of the military allowed their students taking collegiate programs to participate in sports.[4]

On the high school level, even though coaches expressed fears that they would lose any player 18 years old or older, both Granby and Maury continued to use Foreman Field. The games were usually staged on weekend nights despite the call for blackouts to prevent German U-boats, lurking in the Atlantic, from silhouetting intended victims on the shipping lanes. Attendance ran to 7,500 in at least one encounter early that year but tapered off as the season progressed, as both schools fell out of contention for the championship of the Virginia High School Athletic and Literary, the official overseer of state athletics for many years. The city's inability to provide sufficient police protection became a problem, causing at least one suggestion that high school games be transferred to Sunday afternoons to replace the Dixie League ones that no longer existed. But nothing came of that idea.

Attendance at some scholastic events did fairly well through the rest of the war, possibly because of the population buildup. Maury attracted 6,000 fans in tying Petersburg High School on a Saturday afternoon, but with the Commodores headed for another state championship that year and the big game against the Comets moved to Thanksgiving, some 12,000 appeared at the site. A slightly smaller audience (10,000) watched Granby romp over Maury in 1944, also on Thanksgiving. Spectators got the chance to participate in some gambling related to the Sixth War Bond drive. Granby, led by lefty Chuck Stobbs, won handily, as it continued a winning streak that would last another two years.

As for the collegians, in 1943 the Cavaliers (at some point becoming the V-12) succumbed to North Carolina Pre-Flight, 54-7, before 15,000 (one source says 12,500) on Thanksgiving Day. The Pre-Flight squad included Art Jones, who had recently played professionally with Pittsburgh. In October, North Carolina State bumped William & Mary, 19-2, before a "colorful gathering" of 12,500, but the Indians had won earlier in October before 10,500 over Maryland. Neither the military draft nor restrictions on travel during the war closed down collegiate competition, and scholastic football seemed on the rise.

After the war, high school ball quickly reached a higher level of intensity. In November 1945, a crowd of 16,000 watched the Comets whitewash the Commodores, 52-0, as Granby won its 21st straight game. Despite potential dim outs on night ball due to the strike of coal miners, 25,000 (a then-record number for Foreman Field) watched Granby win, 46-13, over Wilson in 1946. Later that year Foreman Field was the site of one of the most important showdowns in all of Hampton Roads' history when on Thanksgiving the undefeated Granby Comets overcame the Maury Commodores, 27-12, to win the state football championship before 26,000.

On the fifth anniversary of the Japanese attack on Pearl Harbor, Granby took on undefeated Clifton High School of New Jersey, the Passaic Valley champion, in the first Oyster Bowl. This bowl game, sponsored by local Shriners, would become an annual event. With backs Chuck Stobbs and Barney Gill, center Hank Foiles–future major league pitcher, standout back with the University of Virginia, and National League catcher, respectively–the Comets squeezed out a touchdown for a 6-0 win before 21,000, with all seats sold. The asking price of $2 for regular seats and $12.50 for special reserved seats brought in $50,000, most of which went to help crippled children. Such bowls, named for fruits, flowers and other crops, proliferated in post-World War II America. The idea for an "Oyster Bowl" originated with E. E. Turpin of the Norfolk Advertising Board, who in a speech before the Cosmopolitan Club in 1940 urged the creation of a four-year college in Norfolk as well as a game like the Rose Bowl–but named for the lowly oyster.[5]

That such a large number watched these games suggests that the original 18,000 seating capacity had changed somewhere along the way. Knowing they could attract big crowds, the Shriners purchased portable bleachers that were stored under the stands and put up behind the end zones at game time. In the late 1940s, Walter Hoffman chaired a city-appointed committee that recommended that the city lease Foreman Field from the college. This action came about because of complaints from the Norfolk Sports Club, whose members believed the college had not been transparent in its disposition of rentals and concessions funds. In a speech to the club, Hoffman reminded its members of the high costs of maintenance at the stadium. Based on the committee's recommendation, in 1950 the city rented the site from the college for 25 years. At the same time it forgave the college what remained of the original loan for the land. In 1953, the city council came up with $65,000 to put in 5,300 seats on the south end of the field. Four years later, the city paid for another 3,000-plus seats in the north end. These steel bleachers, with wooden benches on them, brought total permanent seating to around 26,000. The college's only concern about these additions was that the time for debt amortization not exceed the time of the lease. Clearly, Norfolk's municipal leaders wanted to control the stadium but did not want to own it.[6]

The Shamrocks returned for a few seasons after the war. Facing clubs like the Newport News Builders, they again played on Sundays. Probably the single most highly attended professional game of this era took place in September 1946, when the local professionals took on the highly favored Washington Redskins, who easily "scalped" them. Before the game, "Slingin' Sammy" Baugh, one of the greatest quarterbacks in National Football League history, was pictured on the sports page attired in Native American regalia. On the field, Baugh had little difficulty riddling the Shamrock defense with precise passing. "Pistol Pete" Sachon, a little All-American from Catholic University in 1940 and a Shamrock in 1941, tried to quarterback Norfolk to a touchdown, but to no avail. Walter Halme, Walter Lakin and Hickey Smith, all former Braves, were all listed on the program for the game, but the game account does not mention any of their names. Auctioneer Maury Riganto, another former Division player, announced the game over the loudspeaker. It was not a particularly good year for the Shamrocks, who also lost to the Richmond Rebels, 27-0, with "Artful Art" Jones guiding the winners, before but 2,500.[7]

Military ball attained new heights, as 14,000 assembled to watch the Little Creek

Amphibians subdue Fort Pierce, Florida, when they stopped quarterback Johnny Lujack, a former and future star at Notre Dame. A week later, on the last Saturday in November, 1945, the Amphibians shut out Florida University before around 7,000, the only appearance of a major college football team at Foreman during 1945 and 1946.[8]

Military football attracted more attention after the war than it had during it—at least at Foreman Field on Sunday afternoons. Military elevens varied greatly in quality, with some not likely to hold their own against small-college junior varsities. Others, with former professional players and college stars, were among the finest football clubs in the nation. In 1948 at Foreman Field, the Quantico Marines prevailed over the San Diego Leathernecks, 21-0, before 18,000 to win the U.S. Naval championship. The March of Dimes (to combat polio) and Navy Relief split the net gate receipts.

The "Red Feather Bowl" began in 1949, the name derived from the symbol of the Community Chest (later known as United Way). Admiral Ralph O. Davis, once a commandant of the Fifth Naval District, introduced the idea of having a military bowl in support of local charities. That year, Little Creek triumphed over the Bluejackets from the Navy Base, 17-13, before more than 14,000. Although the money donated by fans that year did not amount to much, the activity coincided with the highly-publicized fall drive of the charity. In another contest that year, Quantico took the Mid-Atlantic title game from the Little Creek Amphibians, 24-0, before 8,000. In 1954, the Navy Tars overcame the Amphibious Forces, 27-14, for the first time, before 14,000. This particular bowl continued for nearly a decade, with the Tars and Gators playing each other. The latter won seven of nine contests. George Welsh (future Navy and Virginia coach) won plaudits in a losing effort in 1956 for the Tars. Coached by Jack Cloud, the Bluejackets reigned supreme in 1957. The last bowl game featured the Tars and the Fort Lee Travelers, representing the Navy and Army respectively. Ten thousand showed up for this game, easily won by the Tars, but the money donated failed to come near the amount collected the previous year, when tickets were sold.[9]

On the college front, one game was played in 1947, a late-September triumph by William & Mary over Davidson, led by former Granby coach Bill Storey, and including some Norfolk boys in the lineup. William & Mary, however, had one-time Maury standout Jack Cloud as a sophomore, and though the Wildcats fought the Indians to a standstill in the first half, the Tribe unleashed its offense to win going away in front of about 10,000 fans.

In October 1948, college football received a big boost when the Shriners renewed their Oyster Bowl commitment, with collegians now providing the competition. The banning of post-season play by those in charge of high school football forced the Shriners to turn to colleges for their special bowl. On the day of the first collegiate contest, the front-page headline read: "Oyster Bowl Fever Grips Norfolk." The event occurred as U.S. airplanes offset the Soviet Union's attempt to blockade Berlin. Although in the midst of a presidential campaign, Strom Thurmond, running as the Dixiecrat (segregationist) candidate, sat on the William & Mary side of the stands at Foreman Field with his attractive 22-year-old wife, a row or two back from Governor Bill Tuck. Although the speculation was that Tuck might endorse Thurmond, both agreed not to play politics that day; even so, the South Carolinian could not resist stating his opposition to the Federal Fair Employment Practices Commission during a press session at halftime.

Jack Cloud and George Hughes, both former Maury men, led William & Mary over VMI, 31-0. At the time the Indians were the best collegiate club in the state, having played in the Dixie Bowl in Birmingham the previous January. The chair of the Shriner fund drive said the attendance and receipts were well beyond his "fondest expectations," presumably meaning the net receipts were over $50,000.[10]

In early December 1948, the first "Fish Bowl" occurred, with Hampton Institute upsetting favored Wilberforce College from Ohio, 20-19, in an exciting contest between two black teams. A driving rain kept the crowd down to about 4,000. Over the next decade, with the exception of two years, Foreman Field housed the bowl sponsored by the Arabia Shrine, which raised money for research on tuberculosis and other diseases. In 1954, the Maryland State Hawks won over North Carolina A&T before 6,000. Most of the teams that played in Foreman in this bowl during the 1950s represented what was then the Colored Intercollegiate Athletic Association. In 1959, the Shriners started to use Frank D. Lawrence Stadium in Portsmouth, but they later returned to Foreman Field.

North Carolina State won the 1949 Oyster Bowl, beating Virginia Tech, 14-13. That same year, the Community League introduced a Halloween Bowl. Neither State nor Tech had won a game that year, but the Shriners sold more than 21,000 tickets. The next year (1950), William & Mary stunned favored State by a 34-0 margin in the bowl, thus ending a losing streak before some 15,000.

Under the right circumstances, high school games involving Granby, Maury or Wilson might pretty well fill up a major part of the stands. Interest in high school ball dropped off in 1947 after an enthusiastic start, when Roanoke High School beat Granby before 9,000. Granby's winning streak had ended the previous Christmas to Lynn (Massachusetts) High School in Miami in a game considered as the championship of the eastern part of the United States.

Some 10,000 watched a 1948 game, with Maury winning over Wilson, 12-0, on a Friday night at Foreman Field, while Granby caved in to Hopewell in front of 7,000 that same year. The Commodores crushed the Comets in 1948, 35-0, before 15,000. On Thanksgiving 1949, Maury got by Granby, 7-0, in a thriller before 12,000. That season, Maury also upset Petersburg and tied the Newport News Typhoons (before 8,000), both on Friday nights.

Interest in high school football received a serious blow in 1958, when the state mandated that Norfolk's three all-white public high schools close rather than allow blacks to attend. Curiously enough, even though the schools were closed through the entire fall and beyond, the former students still played football. Maury athletes attended school at a nearby synagogue under the direction of principal A. Rufus Tonelson, who had played baseball and basketball for the Norfolk Division in the early 1930s. Over time, however, many players made arrangements to attend other schools or simply stopped coming to practice, thus depleting the squad. The same thing occurred at Granby, but less so at Norview High School, which continued to win most of its games. Nonetheless, both Maury and Granby played out the season, before a handful of spectators in several games. On Thanksgiving, around 5,000 came out to watch two teams that combined had only three wins. Granby prevailed, 31-0. Bands played, people cheered, but the schools being rooted for, in a sense, no longer existed.[11]

A throng of 20,000 came to Foreman Field in 1966 to see the powerful Comets overcome Maury, 14-7, in their annual Thanksgiving encounter. Only 8,000 came out the week after Thanksgiving, when Granby again won the state title, this time against Andrew Lewis High School. But interest in scholastic football began to drop off in the late 1960s, sometimes due to inclement weather, weak teams, or both. Only 5,000 saw Maury inflict a 54-26 loss on Granby on a very cold Thanksgiving in 1970. The introduction of a scholastic playoff system forced the cessation of playing on Turkey Day, but that trend could also be attributed to the popularity of pro football on that special occasion. Some writers lamented the end of collegiate and scholastic football on the day, a practice that had started around the beginning of the century.

In the 1950s and 1960s, Shriners brought in creditable opponents, including some of the top stars nationally, often representing different sections of the country. Especially successful were the Oyster Bowls involving the Naval Academy. It took a major effort, particularly the persistence of Walter Hoffman, to convince naval authorities to participate. In 1954, in the aftermath of Hurricane Hazel and as the nation's teenagers were "rocking around the clock," George Welsh guided the Navy split-T in a romp over Duke before 28,000. That set the record for the bowl and the stadium, and exceeded the regular seating capacity.

Standard practice for the Naval Academy was to send the midshipmen down the Chesapeake Bay on naval ships to Lambert's Point, after which they made their way to the field and occupied a big block of seats in the stands. Through the efforts of the Shriners of Khedive Temple, ticket sales, even in inclement weather, topped 30,000. In 1957 quarterback Tom Forrestal excelled for Navy in overcoming Georgia. Both teams were spared the Asian flu, a lethal illness that forced the cancelation of some collegiate games that year.

A monster turnout of 32,169 in 1958, when Tulane upset Navy, prompted the city to look into the possibility of adding 10,000 more seats to Foreman Field by building a horseshoe-shaped addition to replace the metal bleachers at the south end of the field. But despite columnist Bill Cox's excitement about that possibility, or of building a new stadium that would hold more than 50,000, nothing came from either idea.

In 1959, Syracuse was the best team in the nation, featuring the great Ernie Davis (winner of the Heisman Trophy in 1961). They easily overcame Navy, which was minus their explosive running back, Joe Bellino. Davis was one of only three blacks to participate in the game. Art Baker and John Brown were the other two, both on the Syracuse team. Baker, a junior fullback who also played defense, scored on a long interception and on a 13-yard run. Davis won the Mel Blassingham Award as the game's best player. That these three blacks were the first to break the color line for a football game in Foreman

Field received little fanfare by the Norfolk press. Columnist Cal Jacox of the African-American-focused *Norfolk Journal and Guide* said only that local whites accepted the achievements of Davis and Baker with obvious approval.[12]

With Joe Bellino (another Heisman Trophy winner) leading the way, Navy beat Southern Methodist in 1960. Despite rain, the Shriners sold more than 32,000 tickets and fully 30,000 showed up. In 1962 Roger Staubach, a "slim, awkward" sophomore quarterback, led the Middies to a surprisingly easy win over the Pittsburgh Panthers; the next year, the future Heisman winner returned and, surprisingly, had a difficult time in besting VMI, 21-12.

In a 1967 game between two local favorites, Duke edged Navy before 30,000. When Navy played at Foreman Field, it was not a question of if the game would be a sell out, but rather how soon that would happen. And the Shriners routinely turned over $100,000 to their hospitals. "Strong Legs Run that Weak Legs May Walk" became the well-known slogan.

In the 1970s, as Americans weathered an unsatisfactory outcome of the Vietnam War, two oil embargoes, the Watergate scandal, and a tendency for negatives like unemployment, poverty, and skyrocketing prices, attendance at the Oyster Bowl started off weakly. Maryland and North Carolina, both respectable Atlantic Coast Conference teams, attracted far fewer than 20,000 in what became a blowout for the Tar Heels. The next year, a Clemson field goal against Duke before 20,000 was the game's only score. When Duke returned in 1972 to win over Navy, 17-16, Foreman Field hosted a full house (26,000).

A lopsided Terrapin win over the Blue Devils the next year brought in 20,500. In 1974 the number went back up to 24,000 as Maryland "shelled" Duke again. As writer Jerry Reed heard someone say, "One small step for Maryland, and one giant step backward for Duke." Two non-ACC teams vied in 1975, as 25,000 watched Virginia Tech slug out a 17-0 win over William & Mary.[13]

After a major upset in 1976, when VMI outplayed the University of Virginia, 13-7, William & Mary got by East Carolina University in the loser's first appearance in the bowl, 21-17, in 1977. The most memorable action of that game took place when Jim Johnson, an elderly former coach of the Carolina school, bolted from the sidelines at the 2-yard line to tackle Tommy Rozantz as the Tribe quarterback was sweeping toward the end zone. Tidewater folks talked about "the tackle" for years, usually sympathizing with the old man and commenting about his adept tackle. A year after it occurred, reporter Abe Goldblatt interviewed Johnson and reported that he was a long-time school principal who not only coached East Carolina back in the 1940s, but had also played for them in the 1930s. That means he had most likely tackled a player dressed in green on Foreman Field before—then legitimately—when he played against the Division in a 1937 loss. Whether he had a flashback from 40 years before when he tried to stop the William & Mary quarterback is not known.[14]

In 1980, Virginia Tech, headed to the Peach Bowl under Coach Bill Dooley, beat back VMI, 21-6. The Keydets shut out The Citadel in 1981, just before reconstruction of Foreman Field commenced. The next year, with renovations done just in time, Tech overcame the Keydets before a crowd slightly larger than a full house. This took place at a time when the national unemployment rate topped 10 percent due to the recession under President Ronald Reagan. (Curiously, the rate of joblessness was high when Foreman Field was first built and apparently will be in 2009, when it opens after another renovation.)

Attendance dropped to 20,000 in 1983 as William & Mary upended Yale University, the Eli's first and only visit to the area. Tech returned as a winner the year after that, with 24,000 watching the great Bruce Smith, who told everyone that he became a Hokie because he saw them play in a previous Oyster Bowl. But despite the recruiting advantages for participants, the combatants in 1985 were two elevens of division I-AA of the NCAA; Richmond defeated James Madison, before a fair crowd of 17,000. In 1986, the Temple Owls upset Tech in front of 23,500. After that year, only I-AA colleges like The Citadel and VMI, with smaller squads of scholarship players than more prestigious schools, could be persuaded to participate in the classic. The more well-known programs had less incentive to come because their much bigger stadiums were now more often filled to capacity.

The Naval Academy, once capable of making the sale of tickets easy for the sponsors, did not participate any more; nor did ACC elevens. Through 1988, when The Citadel ground game produced a 31-20 win over VMI in what had come to be called a "Military Classic," attendance remained in the 20,000 range. But a William & Mary triumph over Boston University brought in but 13,500.

Despite the lack of full houses or even full stands, the Shriners kept up the Oyster Bowl tradition into the 1990s. VMI, which played in two of the last three bowls of the

1980s, remained one of the opponents into the 1990s. Its football program, however, had fallen on hard times. The Keydets lost the next six contests in Foreman Field, and with one exception (a 17-14 loss to The Citadel), by lopsided scores. In that skein, William & Mary and the Citadel alternated in their triumphs, separated once by a University of Richmond blowout.

In 1995, the last Oyster Bowl game was played at Foreman Field. Georgia Southern, one of the best in I-AA, interred VMI and, in a sense, the bowl. At that point, the Oyster Bowl no longer produced its annual pearl and was discontinued. As Jimmy Howard, the Shriner then in charge of running the bowl, explained, declining or static attendance was not the only problem. The stadium, despite the renovations of 1982, still had problems of aging. Moreover, Old Dominion now charged $10,000 rent, about double a former rate. Just bringing in game officials cost $5,000, not to mention transportation costs for the participants. Even the city of Norfolk piled on about an average $8,000 in amusement tax, which to say the least was not very funny. And so, with skyrocketing costs and inadequate quarters, the Shriners suspended their bowl. Over nearly a half century, the Oyster Bowl had attracted more than 1.1 million spectators and netted around $3 million for crippled and burned children. Its pre-game parades and other festivities had become an annual tradition for thousands of area residents and tourists. After a three-year hiatus, the Shriners brought the bowl game back on the Peninsula, featuring schools like Newport News Apprentice and Division III opponents.[15]

Based on the success of the Oyster Bowl, other organizations tried their hand at sponsoring college games, especially in the 1950s and early 1960s. Some of these efforts, usually for some charitable purpose, did well; others did not. The Optimist Club conducted at least one college contest at Foreman Field. In 1954, North Carolina State upset William & Mary, 26-0, even though the loser was favored to win by three touchdowns. A seven-touchdown reversal must be some sort of record. The crowd of 12,000 pleased the sponsors and helped the Optimists collect funds for Boys Clubs, their slogan being "Friend of the Boy."

The Norfolk Sports Club probably took a financial bath when heavy rains undermined a Tech-Wake Forest encounter in 1958, but a "Civitan Bowl" that year, won by VMI over Virginia, brought out around 15,000, the beneficiary being the Foundation of Mentally

Retarded and Handicapped Children. The Civitans sponsored a 1959 contest, wherein VMI cruised by William & Mary, 26-7, but a only a "small crowd" of 6,500 could be enticed to help children with mental or physical ailments. Roman Gabriel, then a sophomore quarterback at North Carolina State, appeared in an exciting win over VPI in the "Good Neighbor Bowl," put on by the Norfolk Sports Club the next year before 11,000. Also in 1960, when Norfolk was at its peak population (of more than 300,000 residents) and won an award as an "All-American City," the Norfolk Sports Club, under the leadership of former Division center Maury Riganto, persuaded the University of Virginia and William & Mary to play their annual contest at Foreman Field.

With these two natural rivals both having a considerable following in the area, columnist Bill Cox figured at least 10,000 would show up, even though the game was played in September, less than prime time for a football contest. When fewer than 6,000 paid their admissions, Cox forecast a poor future for any more such experiments and also for any chance the city might build a larger facility. Norfolk, instead, would turn its attention to building an indoor arena for college basketball, ice hockey and the like.[16]

A new dimension surfaced in 1965, when the Norfolk Neptunes—thankfully they did not use the name first suggested, the "Gobs"—revived interest in professional football. In April that year, a Norfolk ownership group led by general manager Jim Dunn obtained a franchise in the Continental Football League, the tenth team accepted. League officials had serious doubts about whether Norfolk, with its poor reputation for supporting collegiate contests and unimpressive numbers (about 5,000 per game) for the old Shamrocks, could sustain a program here. But this exciting, offensive-minded brand of minor league football caught on.

Tom Garrett, one of this book's authors, served as a ball boy and locker-room attendant with the Neptunes as he grew from a junior at Wilson High School to a junior at Old Dominion University. From the first game on August 17, 1965, when the Neptunes lost to the Fort Wayne Warriors, 24-17, Garrett developed "a love affair" with the team. He recalls the different teams from the ever-changing league: the Charleston Rockets, Philadelphia Bulldogs, Brooklyn Dodgers, Montreal Beavers, Toronto Rifles, Hartford Charter Oaks, Wheeling Iron Men, Richmond Rebels, Indianapolis Capitals and the Jersey Jays.

Garrett remembers a game on October 10, 1966, when the Brooklyn Dodgers came to Foreman Field with their general manager—pioneering baseball player Jackie Robinson—watching from the sidelines. But he especially remembers the rivalry with the perennial power in the league—the Orlando Panthers, led by quarterback Don Jonas. On August 22, 1970, he listened to Norfolk defensive players in the locker room before a game against the Panthers threaten to "flatten" Pat Palinkas, because by holding the ball for her husband to kick extra points, she was making a mockery of the game. After Orlando converted one extra point and the local crowd cheered, Orlando switched to another holder and the crowd booed.

Some fan favorites included Donnie Floyd, Junior Edge, Dan Henning, Joe Hightower, Art Zachary, Herman Driver, Paul Duda, Otis Sistrunk and "Boom Boom" Brown. Some of these men and many other players remained in the area after the team ceased play. Garrett also vividly recalls cheerleaders, including Debbie Shelton. An ODU student who won the Miss USA crown and was runnerup in the 1970 Miss Universe contest, Shelton went on to play J. R. Ewing's mistress in the television show *Dallas*.

The Neptunes often attracted fairly large crowds. Over their five home games in 1965, the club averaged well over the magic number of 10,000, as the club held onto second place in the league's Eastern Division. In 1967, a record 19,761 paid customers witnessed a 35-31 Saturday night win over the Orlando Panthers. The lowest turnout that year fell just below 10,000. The club posted an 11 and 3 record, losing the championship game. During their existence, more than 600,000 attended Neptune games. Garrett credits part of the reason for the team's popularity to management's decision to sell tickets at a reasonable price, including ticket sales for only $2 for ODU students who often sat in blocks in the end zones.

Gary Glick was the team's popular first coach. He was assisted by Maury High grad George Hughes, a former star safety for the Pittsburgh Steelers who owned a hardware store in Ocean View. Hughes would later become co-coach of the Neptunes. When Glick left the franchise to return to business in Colorado, Hughes became head coach.

When the Continental League went under, Norfolk joined the Atlantic Coast Football League and carried on through 1970 under the ownership of Tidewater Professional Sports. In 1971, Pennsylvania businessman Ed Gruber bought the franchise and hired Ron Waller as general manager and coach. Although Gruber had hopes of obtaining a

National Football League franchise, such aspirations proved well out of reach. Average attendance dropped a bit below 10,000, in part because of the sameness of the competition. The league had only four teams: the others were the Roanoke Buckskins and two clubs from Connecticut—Bridgeport and Hartford.

Foreman Field also was used during this time for NFL pre-season games. These games not only brought in talented players, they allowed the press an opportunity to remind readers of the number of Oyster Bowl participants who became pro stars in the National Football League. The Kiwanis Club sponsored these games, usually held on Saturday evenings. As with the Oyster Bowl, net receipts went to charity. In 1965, Lou Michaels kicked four field goals to help Baltimore Colts ax the Washington Redskins, 33-23, before a record crowd of 22,117. The next year the Redskins gave way to the Monsters of the Midway (Chicago Bears), with more than 20,000 watching.

In 1970, when the cost of putting on the game reached $80,000—double the initial price—the Kiwanis gave up trying to entice NFL teams to come to Foreman. In addition, attendance dropped noticeably if the Redskins were not involved. When Pittsburgh played the St. Louis Cardinals in 1969, fewer than 14,000 watched a game that cost the Kiwanis $70,000 to stage. So in 1970 the service club called on the Neptunes to play a pre-season game, which they conducted victoriously against their great rivals, the Orlando Panthers, and charged the Kiwanis only $27,000. That was the game mentioned by Tom Garrett, where a woman held a football for a placekick.

These games allowed the philanthropic organization to support their favorite charities, which over the years included $130,052 for Old Dominion University's Child Study Center and $80,000 for a variety of worthy causes, including the Florence Crittenden Home and the Little League.

In 1965, the Norfolk Sports Club brought in two teams from the American Football League that would soon join the National Football League—the New York Jets and the Boston Patriots—for a pre-season showdown in late August. The Jets had the much-heralded Joe Namath, but the former University of Alabama star failed to impress most of the 9,200 fans. The other Jets did, however, as they rolled to a 17-0 win.[17]

When professional football faded, Norfolk State University began to play most of its home games at Foreman Field. That institution had started in the late 1930s as a private school under the aegis of Virginia Union College in Richmond, with the help of student aid from the federal government. In 1945, the school became public as the Norfolk Division of Virginia State College in Petersburg, at which time it also fielded its first football team. For some years it played at a low level of competition, but then graduated to playing teams like Virginia State and Hampton University in the prestigious Colored Intercollegiate Athletic Association in 1962. Norfolk State played in Tar Park (a.k.a. High Rock and later Myers Field) until the mid-1950s, when that stadium, no longer needed for minor-league baseball with the death of the Piedmont League, was razed.

After playing at Portsmouth's Lawrence Stadium and at Community Field, a privately owned facility not far from the Norfolk State campus, the college began to play a few games at Foreman Field. Included was one against the great Grambling team in the early 1970s that attracted 15,000. But another contest that year, against archrival Hampton University, brought in only 1,500. Attendance depended a great deal on the quality of the team and the competition, but it could be pretty disappointing, as when a weak 1973 Spartan eleven gave way to Eddie Robinson's Grambling, 32-6, before but 6,000. High attendance that year reached 13,000, when the Virginia State Trojans shut out Norfolk State.

The next several years, however, brought winning clubs under coach Dick Price and with them, higher attendance. In 1974, in his first year after taking over as coach from Bob Ledbetter, Price's team won all its CIAA games, including four at Foreman Field, where crowds ranged from 6,000 against Fayetteville State to 9,500 against Elizabeth City State. In the last home game of the season, however, as the Spartans moved closer to their first CIAA championship, more than 16,000 saw a win over Virginia Union of Richmond. That year, Norfolk State lost three out-of-conference contests (none at Foreman Field) to North Carolina A&T, Grambling and Tuskegee by a combined total of nine points, the last-mentioned as a result of a blocked punt, 15-14, in Atlanta in the Gate City Bowl.

Even though Price's crew never quite matched the perfect CIAA record of the 1974 season, they usually played an exciting brand of ball and drew fairly large crowds. More than 17,000 watched the Spartans pummel the Hampton Pirates in November 1976. Later that year, either 18,000 or 22,000 (depending on which part of the newspaper one reads), witnessed a win over Virginia Union. In the late 1970s, playing four or five home games at Foreman Field, the Spartans attracted crowds ranging from a few thousand to close to a full house.[18]

In the meantime, high schools made occasional use of the facility. When Met Park in the eastern part of the city became available in the early 1970s, several high school games, including those of Maury, were transferred there. Foreman Field remained the site for some important games, but attendance never came near the levels that it had formerly attained.

In the mid-1970s, in the wake of suggestions that major changes needed to be made in high school football, *The Virginian-Pilot* ran a poll on the various proposals in its "Compass" section. Only a few people bothered to respond, but from the letters that were published with the poll results, one finds far-ranging ideas about the issue. A clear majority wanted to refurbish Foreman Field and a minority wanted to make Met Park more football friendly. Only one person voted to do both and a handful did not want to do either. One man succinctly stated the matter by writing: "Build a stadium at Met Park. Tear down Foreman Field." One ODU faculty member thought city money should not go to sports at all while Dr. Franklin Ross Jones, former dean of the School of Education, thought Foreman Field should be made over and Met Park improved as well, with a view of adding football at ODU.

One enemy of taxation thought frills like football stadiums should not be subsidized, at least until the council could lower the tax rate. A resident near Foreman Field wished for the destruction of the stadium, so that those attending games would no longer litter the landscape, create parking problems and make so much noise. One writer wanted to renovate Foreman Field and expand parking next to the Larchmont Elementary School by filling in a swamp. A Maury High student urged preserving Foreman Field because he couldn't afford transportation to Met Park, but he also urged public officials not to drain the swamp or do away with the recreational field near the elementary school merely to provide more parking.

Other writers downplayed the violence related to high school games. But that was a serious problem in the early 1970s. Youths took advantage of night high school games to create considerable mischief. They stood on the roofs of nearby buildings, tore up bricks from the Williamsburg Lawn and threw them at campus security, and even beat up residents in nearby neighborhoods, including at least one visiting professor.[19]

Starting in the mid-1970s, the city and the University dealt with the fate of Foreman Field. The city's 25-year lease was due to expire in 1975, and the college administration under President James L. Bugg, Jr. decided to tear down the facility. Several issues led to this decision. The Crosby, Stills, Nash and Young concert on August 17, 1974 (which Tom Garrett attended and describes as the "largest sea of humanity" ever seen on the ODU campus) attracted a crowd of more than 35,000 with tickets priced at $10. It doubtless brought the city some additional revenue, but it did little to help out the college. Its officials let the event take place, but with serious misgivings over crowd control and whether such activity violated the lease. In its aftermath, when several religious groups sought to hold revivals at Foreman Field, the university official again mentioned the clause in the lease that said only athletic and educational activities could be staged at Foreman Field. They also wanted to keep the crowds below 15,000.

Even though few racial or violent incidents marred either the Oyster Bowl or the four or five games Norfolk State played there each fall, the attendance at these few events looked like a weak reason for keeping the stadium. The university even went so far as to put in $47,000 in a proposed state budget for money to raze Foreman Field. One university official told the press that the stadium would be gone by 1980. Land being at a premium, one of several master plans called for putting campus housing on the site.[20]

Over the next several years, a series of extended leases with the city allowed Foreman Field to escape the wrecking ball. When the city found that it did not have enough resources and/or cooperation from other cities to build an outdoor football arena for 50,000 near Met Park, both the city and the college reconsidered the fate of the famous field. Helping to reach this decision was the fact that Norfolk State football gained a greater following. And so Julian Hirst, Norfolk's city manager; Dr. Alfred Rollins, the new president of Old Dominion University; Harrison Wilson, president of Norfolk State; and several other officials, including ODU Athletic Director Jim Jarrett—who had leaned toward renovation rather than removal all along—found a way to save the stadium. With cost estimates for repairing the stadium rising from $600,000 to over $2,000,000 as they worked out the details, the city council agreed to pay for renovating one set of stands for $300,000 (later revised to $400,000), Khedive Shrine came up with around $93,000 to rebuild the south bleachers, and Norfolk State agreed to a one-time rental payment of

$700,000. With some other financial wands, such as student activity fees, the university came up with the remaining amount and the renovation proceeded. The last lease with the city expired on the last day of July 1980. Renovation included replacing the grass with artificial turf and removing the cinder track, which had not been routinely used for some time after Old Dominion dropped track and field.[21]

The 1980s proved to be positive years for Norfolk State football, at least from an attendance perspective. In the inaugural game at the renovated Foreman Field about 15,000 watched Norfolk State get by North Carolina Central. Although most of the fans interviewed about the facility seemed happy with the new turf and the like, at least one fan expressed concern that the location seemed inconvenient and another contended that Norfolk State needed a stadium of its own on campus. Random game selections for the early 1980s show that in 1981 and 1982 some 16,000 saw the Hampton Pirates upset the Spartans, 17,000 watched a win over Winston-Salem, a near full house (25,000) witnessed a game against Howard University (Washington, D.C.), and 19,000 viewed the Panthers of Union rout the home forces. Only 6,500 saw a victory over Bowie State (University of Maryland) in 1983, but 27,500 mostly pleased fans viewed a rout over Howard University in 1984. The 37th annual Fish Bowl, with a 17-0 win over the Elizabeth City Vikings, attracted 22,000.

A special feature of that era of Norfolk State football was the Fish Bowl. The number of spectators proved a bit weak in 1989 (7,089), when Hurricane Hugo discouraged attendance in a game where the Spartans swamped the Elizabeth City State Vikings, 57-0. But given that the game was usually played early in the football season, the turnout was respectable, and allowed the Arabia Shrine to raise money for charity.

Willard Bailey, who had directed Virginia Union to at least two conference titles, was now leading the Spartans. In his first season, 1984, he guided Norfolk State to a CIAA championship. In 1985, around 30,000 (one source says 29,317 and another 30,307) watched the Hampton Pirates hold off the home club, which scored three touchdowns in the fourth quarter, 36-35. The Spartans lost when they decided to go for the win rather than a tie in what was one of the most exciting games ever played at Foreman Field.[22]

Playing an exciting, if not always winning brand of offensive football under Bailey, Archie "Gunslinger" Cooley and Darnell Moore, the Spartans persisted in plying their craft at Foreman Field into the 1990s. In 1990, 30,397 (a Norfolk State record) came to a critical losing encounter with the unbeaten Union Panthers, with Governor Doug Wilder, an alumnus of the winning school, one of the spectators. In the mid-1990s, with quarterback Aaron Sparrow out of Wilson High amassing amazing numbers of passes attempted and completed, Norfolk State continued to be a highly competitive Division II school.[23]

In 1997, Norfolk State completed a campus stadium. Named for their legendary coach Dick Price, the new facility holds some 30,000. More than 26,000 showed up at Foreman Field to watch Norfolk State's last game there—a shutout over Virginia Union. A few weeks earlier, the Spartans got by Delaware State in the 49th Fish Bowl, the last of that classic at Foreman Field.[24]

The year before Norfolk State left Foreman Field, the possibility of moving an existing Canadian Football League franchise from Louisiana to the area stirred up considerable interest about building a new stadium and a lot of negative comments about Foreman Field's inadequacies—from the lack of bathrooms, parking, and backs for seating to the dilapidated state of the press box (especially disturbing to reporters), not to mention the hardness of the artificial turf. *Virginian-Pilot* reporter Harry Minium pointed out that even as an interim stadium, Foreman Field had problems. When plans fell through for the franchise, the field retained its less-than-pleasing characteristics and encouraged some to think it should be torn down.[25]

As of 1997 collegiate games were no longer being routinely played at Foreman Field. Even though it was theoretically available for high school games, few were staged there. The city of Norfolk eventually built a small stadium on a field west of Powhatan Avenue for its schools. ODU's creation of a separate soccer field meant, in effect, that touch football was the only form of the sport being played at Foreman Field. The school's superb women's field hockey teams still played on the concrete-like artificial turf before audiences that rivaled the small number that watched the Norfolk Division eleven play its last home game against Bergen College in 1940.

High school football played a huge part over the years in Foreman Field's history, with regular season games for Maury and Granby as well as Eastern District and Virginia State High School League Championships. (Courtesy of Sargeant Memorial Room, Norfolk Public Library)

In 1946, the first Oyster Bowl game sponsored by the Shriners, was held between Granby High School and Clifton (New Jersey) High School. The Granby Comets would defeat Clifton High, 6-0, in front of 21,000. (Courtesy of Clay Shampoe)

Each Oyster Bowl game was highlighted with a parade that would wind its way through downtown Norfolk and conclude at Foreman Field. This image is of a float and band from the first Oyster Bowl parade. (Courtesy of Sargeant Memorial Room, Norfolk Public Library)

In 1949, in front of 21,00C fans, North Carolina State defeated Virginia Tech, 14-13, in the third Oyster Bowl. (Courtesy cf Sargeant Memorial Room, Norfolk Public Library)

This circa 1950s postcard shows an aerial view of Foreman Field during an Oyster Bowl game. The parking lots around the stadium are packed with buses. (Courtesy of Sargeant Memorial Room, Norfolk Public Library)

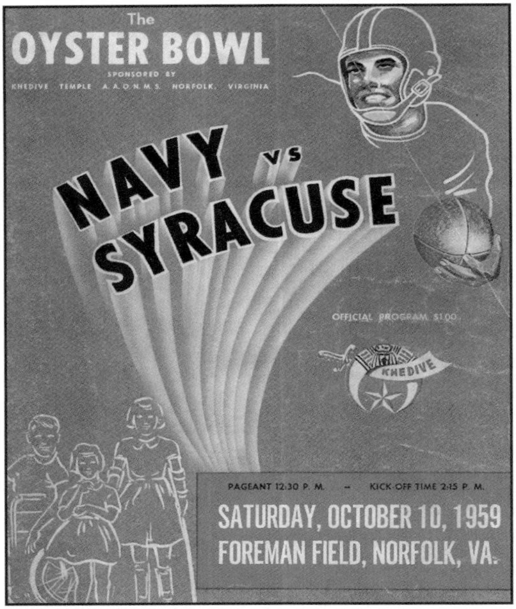

In 1959, Syracuse and Navy met in the 13th Oyster Bowl. Syracuse was led by future Heisman Trophy winner Ernie Davis, who was voted the game's MVP. Syracuse was the only unbeaten and untied major college team in the nation in 1959. (Courtesy of Clay Shampoe)

This aerial view of the halftime program at the 1959 game included a salute to the new state of Alaska. (Courtesy of Sargeant Memorial Room, Norfolk Public Library)

The Washington Redskins led by their quarterback "Slingin' Sammy" Baugh, took on the Norfolk Shamrocks on September 15, 1946. (Courtesy of Clay Shampoe)

Norfolk quarterback Junior Edge leads the Neptunes against the Toronto Rifles in this 1966 Continental Football game. (Courtesy of Clay Shampoe)

On August 17, 1974, a crowd of more than 35,000 jammed the ODU campus and Foreman Field to see Crosby, Stills, Nash and Young in concert. (Courtesy of Sargeant Memorial Room, Norfolk Public Library)

CHAPTER EIGHT

Football or No Football? That Was the Question

Some time after Walter Hodges's departure, leadership at the Norfolk Division eventually fell to Lewis W. Webb, an engineer educated at Virginia Tech. Whenever asked about renewing football, Webb always found reasons to be against it. Football cost money, he'd remind everyone, which the little institution on Hampton Boulevard found difficult to extract from the state via the parent institution in Williamsburg. Had the Division decided to reinstitute the sport after World War II, someone controlling purse strings likely would have said something about affording amenities.

It was also a time when the NCAA tried to create a "Sanity Code" to control payments to students. Even the usually respectable University of Virginia noted that it simply could not possibly field even a halfway competitive team if it had to follow the new rules. Colgate Darden, former governor of Virginia and then president of the University, objected to forcing those who were receiving need-based scholarships to work, but in part to avoid expulsion from the NCAA, Virginia de-emphasized football. That, combined with joining the Atlantic Coast Conference in 1953, made its program uncompetitive for several years.

In 1951, the College of William & Mary experienced an athletic scandal when someone discovered that high school transcripts had been doctored to ensure the admission of five athletes. Officials discovered the typewriter used, but the culprit involved was never disclosed. As early as 1933, it turned out, all such transcripts passed through the Department of Physical Education and the office of the Athletic Director, a procedure ended when the scandal broke.

Soon after, charges surfaced that nine athletes had received credit for physical education courses given during the summer, when most of them were not on campus. Within a short time, football coach Rube McCray, basketball coach Bernard Wilson and even William & Mary President John E. Pomfret were forced to resign. During the heated and very public controversy, the Board of Visitors and members of the faculty traded insults. The Board of Visitors initially advocated that sports remain in a condition conducive to William & Mary teams winning more than they lost, and the faculty pushed to substantially de-emphasize athletics. Technically, whichever side won the argument remains unclear, but William & Mary never again attained the prominence it once enjoyed.[1]

While such events gave impetus to anti-football sentiment at the college in Norfolk, they did not deter some from proposing re-adopting the sport. Sports columnist Bill Cox strongly supported it just after the end of the 1960 season when he reported "a move of better than average firmness to revive football at Norfolk William & Mary." Cox emphasized how much bigger the school ("a big boy now") had become and how many current students had played in high schools or prep schools. An explosion in Tidewater's population meant an even larger college in the future. Some of Scott's former players, "prominent in all walks of life" and active in alumni affairs, generally favored the move, Cox asserted. In addition, Frederick College, a private school in Portsmouth, had just inaugurated the sport and would make a natural rival, as it already did in other sports.

Not only did Cox think the school was ready, but he also believed it could provide "a corrective answer to what ails college football in the Old Dominion." Some of the schools were "old and tired athletically, so to speak," or hemmed in by geographical considerations. Dreaming of a remarkable future for the new program, he foresaw the college becoming a member of the Southern Conference, but within 10 years outgrowing that league, and joining the ACC. Even before hearing about the idea to return football to Foreman Field, he read an article in *Sports Illustrated* magazine regarding the revival of the game at schools like the Johns Hopkins University, where random polls of the student body criticized the administration there for not striving for a higher level of competition.[2]

Whether intending to or not, Cox set the stage for a recurring scenario. Whenever anyone raised the idea of restarting football at the college, someone else would automatically project an image of a great football power emerging almost instantaneously. That vision scared the wits of out of otherwise reasonable people who at the same time had no difficulty envisioning a huge multi-faceted university.

Another columnist of Norfolk's morning daily, George McClelland, picked up the prod to persuade the college to revive the sport. He sometimes slipped the idea into a column on a seemingly different subject, such as when Dr. James Jarrett took over as athletic director and gave a talk to the Norfolk Sports Club, in which he vowed to keep Norfolk on track to field competitive sports and urged community support in that endeavor. At the same time he expressed concern about approaching alumni for too much aid. Near the end of the column, McClelland inserted the notion that Jarrett was "aware that too large a segment of Tidewater knows nothing about Old Dominion save that it has a football stadium and no football team." In reality, that image would soften over the years as the university expanded to the south and Foreman Field became somewhat less conspicuous, particularly so when the nine-story Batten Arts and Letters Building emerged in 1972.[3]

Through most of the 1980s, the question of football resurfaced and at times became a critical issue on campus and in the community. Starting in 1982, some alumni concluded that a decent program could be run for between $1.2 million and $1.5 million. An editorial in the campus newspaper, bemoaning the absence of the sport as fall approached, criticized Jarrett's policy of "selective excellence." As in academics, the university could not do everything and do it well, so it selected a few fields on which to focus.

In sports, that approach had produced successful programs in men's basketball and especially in women's basketball and field hockey. Fielding a football team at a similar level of excellence would most certainly be cost prohibitive, thus the student concluded "we don't have football here and never will." Pointing to the sizeable interest in high school football in Virginia, the editor urged organizing a low-level program, but he lamented that the idea had little chance of success.[4]

Later that fall, students and others began to organize in support for re-introducing football. One writer for the campus paper cited the example of tiny West Georgia College, which had recently adopted the sport and won the Division III national title. She also minimized arguments about endangering existing sports such as field hockey or men's soccer, both of which played on Foreman Field. McClelland returned to the fray, repeating his theme by questioning "the sight of Foreman Field all fixed up with nowhere to go, except to the Oyster Bowl and to a few Norfolk State games." The comment elicited a letter whose writer pointed out that Norfolk State had contributed some $700,000 to help renovate the field and now played four or five home games there every fall, one of which at homecoming attracted a full house of 26,000.

At the time of negotiations over fixing up Foreman Field, nothing had been said about re-creating football at Old Dominion, and doing so, along with the university's new men's soccer and women's field hockey teams might well create schedule complications. Despite McClelland's urgings, it looked as if those who did not want to embark on football at ODU could always find additional reasons not to take such action.[5]

In 1983, one of the campus newspaper's sports editors placed principle blame for not having a team on the students, most of whom did not live on the campus. Creating a program ran the risk of having too little student support. Even though the area possessed some of the finest high school football talent in the nation, it would be some time before the school could attract big names. Before that would happen, students would lose interest.[6]

Harry Minium, a sportswriter for *The Virginian-Pilot*, wrote an open letter to President Al Rollins. Minium pointed to the success of colleges that had recently started football teams. In noting the concern at the college about failure to reach projected enrollment, Minium argued that football would likely attract new students to the campus. He urged the school to start a "bare bones" program without scholarships and later graduate to the I-AA level. Contending that ODU's athletic administration was putting too much emphasis on non-revenue sports, he argued that the area strongly favored football, noting the solid attendance achieved by the Neptunes. Minium did not mention Norfolk State, which attracted full houses on occasion, perhaps because of the possible complications that program presented to starting football at the Hampton Boulevard institution. If finances were such a problem, the writer wanted to know how the institution had come up with money to upgrade Foreman Field and at the same time put $1 million in the new Bud Metheny baseball field. Whatever the merits of Minium's ideas, the ODU administration remained unmoved.[7]

McClelland kept up the pressure on the administration the next fall when he penned a column about Bob Magoon, an ODU faculty member. Magoon hoped to start football at the club level through private donations (about $35,000 would be needed), with the athletic department managing it the same way it would other club sports. The school would compete in the National Collegiate Football Association. The professor clearly would not mind if the school decided to compete on a higher level at some point, noting the success that Dr. Dale Lick, a former member of the ODU administration, had with football as president of Georgia Southern University.[8]

In the spring of 1985, student proponent Bill LaNeeve compared the administration response to the idea of having football to a game of charades, with lots of motion but no one saying anything definite. He pointed out that of 1,500 students surveyed, the majority were willing to have their activity fee raised some $40, and that they felt costs to run a program at the I-AA level should run less than $1 million annually. LaNeeve's faculty friend, Dr. Franklin Ross Jones, inquired among Southern and Yankee Conference Schools about their annual budgets for football. He found, among other things, that almost all of these institutions ran their programs for considerably less than $1,000,000 annually.[9]

That next fall, land developer R. G. Moore offered the University $1.5 million to support a Division I-AA program. The offer stirred up a lot of interest, but by the time the university officially started a fund drive, Moore suffered financial reverses. Robert Stanton on the Board of Visitors, however, kept urging renewal of football. The administration raised the level of necessary support to $5 million and still later to a much higher number. An alumni survey indicated that some 41 percent of graduates would increase their usual giving and another 25 percent said they would start contributing for the first time. A public forum on the last day of January 1986, also produced positive vibes, despite an occasional concern from members of the faculty about recruiting tactics and the like. In light of these findings, the board agreed to assess students an additional $40 for activity fees.

Despite all the negatives about renewing football, in 1987 the ODU Board of Visitors seriously considered a proposal to establish a Division I-AA program. It set an arbitrary fundraising goal of $13.5 million as an endowment to help launch the project. Former basketball coach Paul Webb sought a foundation of financial support from Tidewater's major corporations before going to the general public for the remaining amount. The drive netted but $2,000,000.[10]

Meanwhile, three separate organizations—representing alumni, faculty and students—came up with counterproposals. Public letters revealed a decidedly split opinion about the desirability of any renewal of the sport. Some faculty expressed concern about the dangers to academic standards and others complained about putting a sport above purchasing computers or other campus expenses. Most polls showed student support quite strong, most even willing to accept a hike in the student activity fee. It is doubtful that a majority of the faculty favored the move, even though a pro-football faculty organization had 50 members.

The idea of re-introducing football gained impetus with the arrival on campus of Dr. Joseph Marchello as president. Marchello, with the help of Athletic Director Jim Jarrett, came up with a way around the financial impasse. Because I-AA football was out of the question and Division II football was still too costly in their estimation, Jarrett submitted a proposal for an entirely new classification for NCAA football. After some months, the NCAA agreed to a special classification that, in effect, allowed schools to subsidize athletes with need-based scholarships. Just when it seemed possible to re-start football at the university, the Board of Visitors forced Marchello's removal for reasons unrelated to the status of football. Despite this upheaval, Jarrett planned to proceed in introducing I-AAA level of play. At that time, gifts from alumni and student fees had produced an endowment of $2 million, and even though only 35 corporate sponsorships had been pledged at $5,000 each (less than half of the original goal), ticket and concessional sales and additional student fees meant the proposed program was well within striking distance of the necessary funding to field teams in 1990 or 1991.

Local columnist Bob Molinaro counseled putting off the "Football in 1990" campaign because of the absence of a president and a less than "overwhelming groundswell of enthusiasm." Molinaro, who had never been a strong proponent, urged the plan be postponed at the least. Embarrassing though such a step might be, he maintained that it was necessary to avoid financial chaos.[11]

Although financing remained a major concern, the lack of responses to the new football classification was even more discouraging because it severely reduced the number of opponents ODU could schedule. Former U.S. Senator and interim President William Spong had little time to pursue the matter. His replacement, James V. Koch, had no sympathy for the idea. It looked as if the idea of renewing football had received a death blow, and, indeed, one heard only the occasional mutterings of football enthusiasts trying to determine the fate of funds already pledged by potential donors or accumulated through student fees.

However, the question of whether to have football turned out not to have died. About 15 years after it was seemingly interred, it reappeared. When the university hired Dr. Roseann Runte as the new president, few, if any, football proponents had any idea that she would be the force that would revive the program. One of the members of the Board of Visitors, Moody "Sonny" Stallings Jr., a politically active ODU alumnus, had long wanted to see football at the school. Along with other members of the board, he urged a fresh look at the question. When a Web site survey sent to mostly alumni and students revealed that 92 percent of the more than 6,000 respondents favored football, Runte expressed interest in pursuing the issue.

As the university proceeded with a feasibility study, many of those who had pushed the football idea for over 40 years simply shrugged their shoulders with a look of "here we go again." But when Runte announced her support for the idea, they noticed that she linked the introduction of football as part of a larger program to give the students a full university experience, evidenced by the recent construction of the Ted Constant Center and the nearby University Village, which was soon home to hundreds of students. Still, anyone with a sense of history figured the whole business would soon pass away.

Newspaper reporters and columnists picked up on the issue. Jim Ducibella and Philip Walzer of *The Virginian-Pilot* followed news developments, while columnist Bob Molinaro used the lack of full student support at William & Mary as an example of what could happen in Norfolk. Members of the faculty expressed the usual concerns.

But based on the study, Dr. Runte recommended a plan to the Board of Visitors. Using donations and a rising student activity fee, the school projected it could raise over $24 million to renovate Foreman Field once again. The reconstruction would include an entirely new structure at the south end, where one of the sets of metal bleachers erected after World War II had been torn down after Norfolk State vacated the premises. This new building would include special facilities (such as parking) and seating for corporations and other donors. The highly criticized artificial field would be replaced with one of much higher quality. The board additionally planned for an annual budget, starting at about $4.5 million and more than doubling over the next 10 years.

Suddenly, what seemed like a Herculean task concerning a few million dollars back in the 1980s was coming to fruition at many times that amount. Not only did the board approve the proposal, it passed it unanimously.

Responding to negative comments in an editorial in *The Virginian-Pilot* that had described the process as resembling a "Hail Mary pass," something done with insufficient deliberation, Board Rector Jim Hixon contended that many meetings had been devoted to the issue. He also pointed out that at the same meeting at which the board had approved football, the regular budget increased by nearly $23 million. Likewise, the university had made considerable headway in reaching a campaign goal of $100 million, of which $8 million would go to football. While the amount of money now being allocated to football seemed staggering compared to numbers suggested in proposals in the late 1980s, the growth of the university warranted moving forward.

Costs also included adding three women's sports—volleyball, crew and softball—to help the school be in compliance with Title IX of the Educational Amendments Acts of 1972 (based on the Civil Rights Act of 1964). Costs for these programs and football will be covered in part by a gradual increase in the student activity fee to $10 per credit hour in 2014. A student body numbering well over 20,000, of course, made all this possible.

The administration obtained advice from experts like George Welsh, former coach at the Naval Academy and the University of Virginia, who was quite familiar with Foreman Field. Based on a well-thought-out plan of action, the university hired Bobby Wilder. A graduate in physical education from the University of Maine, where he quarterbacked the Black Bears to the Yankee Conference title in 1986, Wilder served as an assistant coach for a time at Boston College, where he attained a master's in educational administration. Before coming to Old Dominion, he became one of the most highly regarded associate coaches in the country for his alma mater.

Once he arrived on campus, Wilder began the process of creating a staff of eight assistant coaches. Scholarships were awarded to students, who would finish their freshman year before they donned the Old Dominion uniform for the first game. As "red shirt" freshmen, they would be joined by another group of recruits in the fall of 2009, along with junior college graduates, to form the nucleus of the sport's revival.[12]

The game of football and the way of introducing it in colleges h,as markedly changed. Note the contrast between the time required to put a football program in place today compared to organizing one in 1930. Director Edgar Timmerman and Tommy Scott put a team on the field in about two weeks. Scott had about 20 percent of the student body try out for the team; Wilder has a fraction of 1 percent. Wilder will employ a "spread offense," which relies on speed and mismatches to get runners into the open field. Avoiding huddles by using signals from assistant coaches speeds up the game, and overloading tends to create confusion in the defense. Even though some similarities exist between Scott's single-wing formation and Wilder's spread offense, the differences seem greater.

The financial situation has changed considerably over the years. In the early part of the 20th century, the state thought it was doing well by supplementing the school's annual budget by a few thousand dollars, at that time funneled through the William & Mary budget. Now ODU must raise millions of dollars on its own. Strange as the downturn in the economy seems, with unemployment rates similar to those in 1930, the trend will not dilute the celebration of the renewal of ODU's football heritage. Season ticket sales, at one point expected to be in the 5,000-to-10,000 range (some thought 6,000 a realistic number), reached approximately 14,000 months before the season's first game. Because the regular seating will hold fewer than 20,000, ODU officials may decide to install temporary bleachers in the north corner of the end zone. The same technique was employed for well-attended Oyster Bowl or Norfolk State games.

On September 5, 2009, Old Dominion University versus Chowan College marks the renewal of Foreman Field and the start of many new chapters in the legacy of college football on Hampton Boulevard.

So, remember the Braves!

Hail to the Monarchs!

ODU athletic director Jim Jarrett and Colonial Athletic Association commissioner Tom Yeager flank former ODU president Roseann Runte during a party at Foreman Field to celebrate the announcement that football was returning to the university in the fall of 2009. (Courtesy of ODU, Athletic Publications and Creative Services)

The school's ever-popular mascot, Big Blue, shares the same happy opinion as the rabid Monarch fan next to him about the university's decision to once again make football a part of ODU campus life. (Courtesy of Old Dominion University, Athletic Publications and Creative Services)

ODU football coach Bobby Wilder signals a drill during one of the Monarchs' public scrimmages at Powhatan Stadium. From the time he was hired away from the University of Maine, Wilder had a hand in every aspect of the new program, including stadium renovation, uniform colors and design, helmet logos, scheduling and a public-relations campaign that resulted in hundreds of presentations to groups throughout Hampton Roads. He and his assistants even occasionally served lunch in the student cafeteria. (Courtesy of Old Dominion University, Athletic Publications and Creative Services)

Monarchs' defense swarms a ball-carrier during a scrimmage. The offense struggled early with Wilder's spread offense as the coaches juggled personnel, trying to find a solid combination. A goal of the team's second recruiting class was to add some experienced offensive linemen, with an emphasis on junior colleges. (Courtesy of ODU, Athletic Publications and Creative Services)

This scrimmage drew a full house at Powhatan Field, the high school stadium behind the Monarchs' football practice facility. The carnival-like atmosphere outside the stadium included lavish tailgate parties, games and plenty of happy Monarchs fans anxious to assess the team's progress. (Courtesy of ODU, Athletic Publications and Creative Services)

Foreman Field, from the ODU bench. The famous clam-shell bleachers were completely rebuilt by S. B. Ballard Company. The new facility will be named S. B. Ballard Stadium at Foreman Field. Sections were tested for stability by putting dozens of massive water-filled barrels on the bleachers. (Courtesy of ODU, Athletic Publications and Creative Services)

View from the new game-day building, at the stadium's south end. Much of the $24.8 million spent on refurbishing the stadium went into this new construction, which features home-team locker and meeting rooms, an area for recruits and their families, loge seating for 390 and 26 luxury boxes. (Courtesy of ODU, Athletic Publications and Creative Services)

An artist's rendering of what Foreman Field would look like upon completion of its renovation. To the left is a front view of the game-day building, behind which sits one of several new parking garages built to handle the increased traffic. A massive, state-of-the-art scoreboard is located to the far right (not included in this drawing). Crowds of the size depicted are more than a figment of the artist's imagination; all ODU home games were sold out long before practice began in late summer 2009. (Courtesy of Old Dominion University, Athletic Publications and Creative Services)

Appendix I

Norfolk Division Combined Roster 1930–1940

NAMES AND POSITIONS	YEAR(S)	MISCELLANEOUS DATA
Abbott, Cecil Clay/E	'34/'35	145 lbs/Maury/"Skinny"/ "Fred"
Abrams, William/LHB	'30m/'32	149 lbs/5'9"/Bill
Adams/LE	'36	Newport News
Allen, James/G	'37m	170 lbs/Maury
Alvarez, Bill	'34	
Anderson, Bill /E	'33	
Allen, James Wilmer	'37	Maury
Ames, Bill	'30m	Maury
Bagley	'36	
Bacalis, Paul Nicholas/C	'38m/'39	Maury
Baker, Barnabas Bill/G	'39	WWHS/VMI Frosh
Baldwin, Raymond Stuart/RT	'35/'36	Maury/151 lbs

NAMES AND POSITIONS	YEAR(S)	MISCELLANEOUS DATA
Ball, Harry S./RE/LE	'31/'32m/'33	143 lbs/5'11"/Maury
Ball, Littleton Read	'34	Maury
Barham, T.A./G	'37/'38m	168 lbs/Maury
Barnes, Elmo /QB	'33/'34/'35	161 lbs/Emporia
Barnes, Woodrow/RE/QB	'35/'36/'37m	160 lbs/6′/"Specks"/Oceana
Barsell, Berger Edwin/E	'35/'36/'37	160 lbs/Maury
Battaglia, Philip	'34	
Baxter	'30m	
Belkov, Irvin /FB	'33/163	Maury
Bell, Courtney Minor/HB	'33/'34	Maury
Bisschop, Henry Peter	'39	Maury
Blackwell, John/RG	'39/'40	Maury
Bond, "Clipper"/ HB	'32	Hertford HS
Bowden	'33	Manager
Bowen/RG	'30/'31	"Pop"/"Buck"
Brichter, Joe	'38/'39	Tarrytown, NY
Brock, Elwood Emmett/RE	'34	"Andy"/Maury
Brock, Benjamin/DB	'37/'38m/'39	Benny
Brown, John/B	'37m/'38m/'39	155 lbs/"Jack Rabbit"/Maury
Buchanan	'35/'36	
Buell	'33	
Burleson, Bob	'38	
Burton, Jim /LE/LT	'30/'31	164 lbs/injured '30
Byers, Buddy	'39	151 lbs/Philadelphia Eagles
Carlisle	'39	
Carner, George Louis/LG	'32/'34	152 lbs/5'8"/Maury
Cason	'36	Manager
Cavish, Mike/RHB	'32m	180 lbs/Atlantic U

NAMES AND POSITIONS	YEAR(S)	MISCELLANEOUS DATA
Coplan, Oscar	'35	
Carroll, Archie	'36	
Carroll, George/B	'37/'38m	195 lbs/Maury
Chadwick, Lou	'38	Assistant Coach
Chapman, McDonald/ RE/LE	'36	Mac/Maury
Cluverius	'34	Manager
Coble	'32m	"Sugar"/Lynchburg College
Cole, Jimmy	'39	
Colendo, Chris	'37	
Cooper, Adrian Dorsey	'39	WW II KIA
Cooper, James/C	'37m	181 lbs/Elizabeth City
Coppedge, Jack /HB	'34/'35	150 lbs/WWHS/
Cox	'34	
Creech, John/LG	'34	
Crosby b	'40	
Crutchfield	'33	
Cummings	'34/'35	
Cuthrell	'33	
Dailey/T	'33/34	165 lbs/6'
Davis, John/C/G/T	'34/'35	193 lbs
Davis Q.C./LT	'34/'35	160 lbs/South Norfolk HS
Davis, Russell	'38m	
Dee, Jack/E	'39	Notre Dame
Denny, Roger/LT	'33/'34/'35	6'1"/210 lbs/Kempsville HS
Dodson, James Robert/HB	'36/140	Maury
Donovan, Bill	'38	ankle injury
Doyle, Johnny/G/B	'35/'36	150 lbs/5'9"/Oceana HS
Dozier, Wilson/HB/QB	'33/'34/'35	Capt/169 lbs/"Dick"/WW II KIA

NAMES AND POSITIONS	YEAR(S)	MISCELLANEOUS DATA
Dozier, David A./HB	'39/'40	"Pete"/WW II KIA
Drake	'31	
Dryden, Forrest	'39	
Dunn, Bill	'38m	
Dunn, Hewitt	'39	
Durham	'35	
Eames, Willis/RT	'30/'31/'33	167 lbs/6'
Eberly	'35	
Edmonds, Fred/HB/QB	'33/'36	"Speed"
Edmonds, John	'37m	170 lbs
Edwards	'36	
Elsenberg, Irving	'33	
Ellsworth	'35	Manager
Ethridge, Junie	'32m	
Ewell	'34	
Faherty, Bob	'40	
Ferguson, Billy	'39	
Forehand, Clarence/T/RG	'31/'33/'34	Capt/"Sugar"
Foster, Francis/C/T	'37m	175 lbs/"Pete"/H.M.A.
Funk, Mahlon Garlick/B	'37m/'38m/'39	"Maulin"/Maury
Garis, Howard	'33	WWHS
Garrett, Harvey Singleton QB	'34/'35	150 lbs/"Singie"/Maury
Gifford	'36	
Gildner, Douglas/RG	'36/'38m	173 lbs/5′8″/NNHS & Shipbuilder
Godfrey, Walter/B	'35	150 lbs
Goldberg	'35	
Gore, Sunny	'30m	
Griffin, Cecil Linwood Jr./E	'38m/'39	Maury

NAMES AND POSITIONS	YEAR(S)	MISCELLANEOUS DATA
Guy, Buddy	'39	
Guy, Louis/E	'37m	160 lbs/Maury
Gygi, Blois	'37	
Hall, Ed	'30m	
Halme, Walter/FB	'37m/'38	180 lbs/"Swede"
Halstead, Percy	'34/'35	Manager
Hamer, John	'35	
Hamberger, Harry	'30m	
Hanbury, Oliver Ellsworth/E	'40	Maury
Hansen	'36	Manager
Harper, George Wayne/LG	'38	Maury
Harris, W.H./G	'37m	167 lbs/Bill/Oceana HS
Harris, Jack/HB	'37m/'38m	160 lbs/Capt/Augusta M.A.
Harshman, Glenn Warren	'39	"Slug"/Maury
Hassell, John Flemming	'39	Jack/Maury
Hatfield, Joe	'39	
Hawkins, Jack RHB/ FB	'30m/'31/'32	158 lbs/"Ripper"/Blackstone M.A.
Hayman/E	'34/'35	South Norfolk HS
Herbert, Claude	'33	Manager
Herbner, Sam	'36	Wilson HS
Hodges, John David/G	'35	145 lbs/Maury
Hogan, Thomas N./FB/HB	'35	160 lbs/Maury
Holmes, George	'37	Manager
Holsveig, Solomon/G	'37	180 lbs/Maury
Hopkins, Sam/T	'40	
Hoskins, Dick/HB	'40	
Howell, Ned	'37	
Hudgins, Harold Jr./G	'39	Maury

NAMES AND POSITIONS	YEAR(S)	MISCELLANEOUS DATA
Hull, Carl/FB	'39	WW II KIA
Jackson, Edger Earl/C	'34/'35	Maury/157 lbs
Jackson, Frank/G	'35/'36	140 lbs/5′8″/Tom Thumb/Maury
Jackson, J.	'35	
James	'38	Trainer
James, Richard	'39	Rick/KIA
Jarvis, Howard	'37	Manager
Jennings	'36	
Jiminez/LG	'36	
Johnson, Elmer	'30m	
Johnson, Fred/HB/FB	'34	Pensacola, Florida HS
Jones, Allen Talmadge	'39	"Boney"/Maury
Jones, Johnny	'39	Trainer
Jones, Nat	'33	Manager
Joseph, Donald	'37	146 lbs
Joynes	'36	
Kagey, Clarence Cannon/HB	'33	129 lbs/Maury
Karnezis, Gus	'39	
Kaufman, Jeter/RT	'30m /'31	168 lbs/6'
Kaufmann, Albert Roy/E	'39/'40	Maury/ WW II KIA
Keeney	'35	
Kelley, Thomas Woodrow/RE	'32/'35	165 lbs/6′1″/Maury
Kinnard, Robert/B	'39	Moultrie Georgia
Knighton, Jim/RG (Bill)	'37m/'38m	175 lbs/Beckley High
Kruger, Morris/T	'33	222 lbs
Krukin, Irving Harry	'33	Maury
Krukin, Sidney Alexander/LE	'36/'37m/'38m	165 lbs/Maury/Sid
Kyle, Fred/LE	'34/'35	160 lbs/6'/Princeton/WVU Frosh

NAMES AND POSITIONS	YEAR(S)	MISCELLANEOUS DATA
Lakin, Walter,/G	'30/'32	180lbs/WWHS/All-State
Lambert, Hilary/FB	'32	"Pop"/Maury/VPI Frosh
Lau(t)erback/C	'40	
Lewis, Gilford/G	'37m	170 lbs/"Gilly"/Oceana
Lewis, Judd	'35	Manager
Lively, Garland/T	'37m	175 lbs/Churchland
Logsdon, Ralph	'33	
Lowery/RG	'36	
Macon, David Conway Jr.	'37m	155 lbs/5′10″/"Connie"/Maury
Macon, James Barbour/T/E	'39/'40	Jimmy/Maury
Macon, Joseph Ernest	'37	140 lbs/Joe/Maury
Maloney, James Vincent/T	'40	Maury
Marlowe/B	'40	
Martin, Earl/LHB	'30m/'31	"Salt and Pepper" VPI track star
Matthews, Preston/FB	'36	"Ham"/VPI Frosh
Mauch, Milton	'37	160 lbs
Maxey, Terry/QB	'30m/'31/'32m	153 lbs/5'8"/"Little Maxey"/Maury
McCarthy, Morton/G/T	'39/'40	220 lbs/Patty/city am. golf champ
McCloud, Vincent/G	'33	Portlock
McMillan, William Terrell/B	'34/'35	Mac/132/Billy/Maury
Mercer, Heywood/RE	'33/'34/'35	164 lbs./6′/"Ace"/Maury
Miles, Henry/FB	'36	
Miller, Billy /C	'33/'34/'35/'36	150 lbs/5′7″/Capt
Miller, H	'34	
Morgan, Billy	'30/'31/QB/FB	141 lbs/5'5'/South Norfolk HS
Moore, Herbert	'39	KIA
Moore, Jack Eugene Jr./QB/	'39	W&M/Maury
Morrisette, Francis	'30m	Manager

NAMES AND POSITIONS	YEAR(S)	MISCELLANEOUS DATA
Mosier, Manley	'40	
Nance, Pete/B	'35	140 lbs
Nardini, Fred/HB/QB	'39/'40	New Haven CT
Nash	'32	
Nee, Tommy/C	'31/'32	165 lbs/Maury
Nixon, Claiborne/HB	'36	Duke Frosh/Elizabeth City
Odell	'30m	
Oden, Monte/RE	'38m	
Oliver, Keith/line	'32	Kempsville HS
Olson	'40	
Otis, Murrel	'31	
Ottley, William Parker	'30m/'32m	Maury
Ottley, Milton Marchelle RHB	'31/'32	"Mickey"/Maury
Padgett, James/B	'35/'36	140 lbs/Charlotte, NC
Parks, Gorham/C	'30m/'31	153 lbs/5'11"
Patrick/Lloyd RT	'33	Gulf Coast Academy
Peppin	'34	
Peterson, John Francis/E	'39	Johnny/Maury
Pezzella, Vince/C	'38m/'39	155 lbs/Maury
Phillips, Sam	'30m/'31	144 lbs
Pinkney	'37	Manager
Pitt(s), Harry	'35	Manager
Prince	'40	
Provo, Rayford/T	'32	Elizabeth City HS
Phillips, Sam/E	'30 /'31	144 lbs/6'
Pratt, William	'37m	160 lbs/Elizabeth City HS
Preston, Dean	'30m	
Price, Clarkson Monk/G	'40	"Clicky"/Maury

NAMES AND POSITIONS	YEAR(S)	MISCELLANEOUS DATA
Prichard, Arlie	'33	
Priest, Walter /C	'33	
Provo, Rayford/T	'33	185 lbs/Elizabeth City HS/All-State
Pyles, Kenneth Eugene	'39	Maury
Redford, Shelburne Jos./ HB	'33	Maury
Redwood	'33	Woodberry Forrest
Reid, Hugh Sutton	'32	Maury
Reinberg, John	'39	
Reppert, Lee	'38m	
Reveille, Gil	'39	
Richardson, Bob/RHB/G/FB	'32/'33	180 lbs/Maury/Braxton
Richardson, Ira/LG	'32m/'34/'35	145 lbs/"IJ"/"Jake" Churchland HS
Richter, Harry	'40	
Riganto, Maury RT/LT	'36	175 lbs/6'2"/Maury/Aug M A
Rines, Abraham Samuel	'33	Maury
Roberts, Red/G/T	'33/'34/'35	175 lbs/"Bud"/Maury
Robinett(e), Herman A.	'31	170 lbs/6'1"/"Rummy"/Maury/VPI
Rodgers, Bill/LT/B	'37/'38m	235 lbs/Oceana HS
Rodgers, Jim/T	'40	
Root, Joe/HB	'36/'37m	160 lbs/5'7"/Capt/WWHS
Rose/E	'31	123 lbs/5'6"
Rosenfeld, Bill	'37	Manager
Sacks, Sid/HB	'31	159 lbs/Atlantic U
Sadler/T	'31	165 lbs/5'10"
Salomonsky	'34	Manager
Salsburg	'34	
Saunders, Jake/LT	'32	200 lbs/Maury
Segal	'30m	

NAMES AND POSITIONS	YEAR(S)	MISCELLANEOUS DATA
Scherberger, Joe	'39/'40	
Scherberger, Richard	'39/'40	
Shannonhouse, Archie/C	'33	175 lbs/Elizabeth City HS
Shapiro, Bernard/G/C	'39/'40	U of GA/"Bernie"
Shelton	'35	
Shinn, Jack	'38	Manager
Sickle (A. Sichol)	'31	Atlantic U
Sikence	'33	
Simmons, Murrell Otis/LT	'34	"Red"/"Myrie"
Simpson, Fred	'35	Manager
Singleton, John/RE/FB	'31/'33	153 lbs/5'8"/Maury
Small, John French/RT	'34	"Schnozzle"/Maury
Smart, Bill/C	'32m/'33	
Smith, Bruce	'34	
Smith, Louis/E	'36/'37m	160 lbs/"Hickey"/South Norfolk
Snyder, George Waterbury/G	'31	162 lbs/5'9"/Maury
Spence, Charles H./ T/ RB	'33	166 lbs./Maury
Spencer, John/G	'35/'36	160 lbs./"Sonny"
Stell, Henry Edward	'36	Maury
Stewart, Jimmy/RE	'35	Maury/All-State
Stewart, Rob/E	'36	
Sullivan, Jim	'38m	150 lbs
Sutton, Bob	'36	
Sutton, Roy Clifton/FB	'39/'40	Maury
Tavss, Norman/B	'37	147 lbs
Taylor	'35	
Tazewell	'37	
Terrill/T	'37	

NAMES AND POSITIONS	YEAR(S)	MISCELLANEOUS DATA
Thomas, Bill/E	'31/'32m	NNHS
Tippett, Bill	'37	135 lbs/Two Harbors
Totty, Ralph	'31	Maury
Tolson, William Everett/B	'38m/'39	Maury
Traetto, Mike/RG	'40	New Jersey
Treakle, Harold	'40	Maury
Turville, William/T	'37m/'38m	179 lbs/WWHS/W&M
Tyler, Edward/T	'37/'38m	
Tynes, Clarence/LG	'39/'40	
Uhle	'34	
Upton, Johnny/FB/HB	'40	Maury
Valentine, Francis M./FB/ HB	'34	"Bumpy"/Maury
Vance, Ernest A./LT/RT	'36	195 lbs/5′9″/"Chubby"/ WWHS
Vann	'30m	
Walker, Billy	'30m	Christ Church School
Walker, Clinton/LG	'31/'32/'33	"Jack Okie"/Maury/W&M Frosh
Walker, Rhea Lee/HB	'32/'33/'34	155 lbs/Maury
Warren, Elwood/T	'39	WWHS/W&M Frosh
Wergley, Oscar	'37	150 lbs
West, Bill/C	'40	
Wescott, Albert	'38	170 lbs/"Mac"/Holy Trinity/Aug M
White, Saunders (Tom)/RT	'31/'32m/'33	"Clown"/"Tarzan"/NN Shipbuilder
Wilcox/HB	'40	"Max"
Williams	'34	
Williamson, Thomas Jr.	'32	Maury
Wilbur, George	'39	
Wilson, Frank "Junie"/LHB	'31/'32	Capt./Maury/VMI Frosh
Winston, Louis RG/RT	'32m	190 lbs/Birmingham, AL/Atlantic U

NAMES AND POSITIONS	YEAR(S)	MISCELLANEOUS DATA
Winston, John W./B	'35	145 lbs/Maury
Wood, Bill/T	'34/'35	170 lbs
Wood, Joseph Buchanan	'37	Joe/Maury
Woodson, Bill/B	'37	155 lbs/Western High
Woodward	'40	
Wooten, Earnest	'31	180 lbs/Ernie
Yates, Morgan Gayle/T	'34/'35	230 lbs/Maury

"m" represents "monogram," denoting recipients of football letters

Appendix II

Bowl Games at Foreman Field

DATE	TEAMS AND SCORES				ATTENDANCE
OYSTER BOWLS, 1946-1995					
12/07/46	Granby HS	6	Clifton (NJ) HS	0	21,000
10/15/48	William & Mary	31	Virginia Military Inst	0	21,500
10/29/49	North Carolina State	14	Virginia Tech	13	21,000
11/25/50	William & Mary	34	NC State	0	15,000
10/20/51	Duke	55	Virginia Tech	0	20,000
11/01/52	South Carolina	21	Virginia	14	21,000
10/31/53	Duke	48	Virginia	6	22,000
11/06/54	Navy	40	Duke	7	28,000
11/06/55	North Carolina	32	South Carolina	14	26,000
10/20/56	Pittsburgh	27	Duke	14	27,000
10/19/57	Navy	17	Georgia	14	31,160
10/18/58	Tulane	14	Navy	6	32,169
10/10/59	Syracuse	32	Navy	6	32,000
10/09/60	Navy	26	Southern Methodist	7	32,000

DATE	TEAMS AND SCORES				ATTENDANCE
11/11/61	Duke	30	Navy	9	32,000
10/25/62	Navy	32	Pittsburgh	9	32,000
10/19/63	North Carolina State	15	Virginia	9	31,500
10/16/64	Maryland	10	North Carolina	9	28,000
10/03/65	William & Mary	3	Southern Mississippi	0	24,000
11/12/66	Southern Mississippi	7	North Carolina State	6	26,000
11/11/67	Duke	35	Navy	16	30,000
10/05/68	Duke	30	Maryland	28	25,000
11/15/69	Virginia Tech	48	Duke	12	23,000
10/24/70	North Carolina State	6	Maryland	0	18,200
10/09/71	Clemson	3	Duke	0	20,000
10/28/72	Duke	17	Navy	16	26,000
10/27/73	Maryland	30	Duke	10	20,500
11/16/74	Maryland	56	Duke	13	24,000
11/01/75	Virginia Tech	24	William & Mary	7	25,000
10/30/76	Virginia Military Inst	13	Virginia	7	22,500
11/12/77	William & Mary	21	East Carolina	17	23,000
10/21/78	East Carolina	22	Richmond	14	23,000
10/13/79	Navy	24	William & Mary	7	25,500
11/15/80	Virginia Tech	21	Virginia Military Inst	6	26,000
10/10/81	Virginia Military Inst	14	The The Citadel	0	20,000
11/20/82	Virginia Tech	14	Virginia Military Inst	3	26,500
10/01/83	William & Mary	26	Yale University	14	20,000
10/06/84	Virginia Tech	54	Virginia Military Inst	7	24,000
10/05/85	Richmond	38	James Madison	15	17,000
10/18/86	Temple	29	Virginia Tech	13	23,500
10/31/87	William & Mary	17	Virginia Military Inst	6	20,500
11/12/88	The Citadel	31	Virginia Military Inst	20	13,500
10/14/89	William & Mary	13	Boston University	10	13,000
10/13/90	William & Mary	59	Virginia Military Inst	47	14,000

DATE	TEAMS AND SCORES				ATTENDANCE
10/26/91	The Citadel	17	Virginia Military Inst	14	20,480
10/24/92	Richmond	41	Virginia Military Inst	18	12,500
10/02/93	William & Mary	49	Virginia Military Inst	6	14,000
11/12/94	The Citadel	58	Virginia Military Inst	14	15,520
11/18/95	Georgia Southern	31	Virginia Military Inst	13	8,414

KIWANIS CLASSICS, PRE-SEASON PROFESSIONAL GAMES, 1960-1970

08/27/60	Philadelphia	24	Washington	6	20,132
08/26/61	Baltimore	41	Washington	7	20,302
09/01/62	Washington	29	Chicago	28	28,000
08/31/63	Baltimore	20	Washington	7	22,000
09/05/64	Washington	17	St. Louis	10	20,642
09/04/65	Baltimore	33	Washington	23	22,117
08/20/66	Chicago	24	Washington	10	20,609
09/09/67	Washington	16	Pittsburgh	10	20,615
09/07/68	Washington	24	Pittsburgh	17	17,712
08/16/69	St. Louis	27	Pittsburgh	13	13,815
08/22/70	Norfolk	23	Orlando	14	12,650

RED FEATHER BOWLS, 1949-1958

11/06/49	Little Creek	17	Navy Base	13	14,000
11/12/50	Little Creek	12	Navy Base	7	12,000
11/11/51	Little Creek	31	Navy Base	13	8,000
11/09/52	Little Creek	14	Navy Base	7	13,500
11/08/53	Little Creek	26	Navy Base	6	13,000
10/31/54	Navy Base	27	Little Creek	14	14,000
11/13/55	Little Creek	33	Navy Base	0	–
10/28/56	Little Creek	16	Navy Base	14	8,000

DATE	TEAMS AND SCORES				ATTENDANCE
10/27/57	Navy Base	6	Little Creek	0	8,000
11/08/58	Navy Base	24	Fort Lee	0	10,000

SELECTED FISH BOWLS AT FOREMAN FIELD

DATE	TEAMS AND SCORES				ATTENDANCE
11/11/48	Hampton	20	Wilberforce	19	5,000
09/24/49	Shaw University	13	Hampton Institute	7	12,000
10/14/50	Maryland State	48	Hampton University	12	–
09/28/51	Maryland State	7	NC Central	6	3,500
10/10/53	Maryland State	19	NC A&T	0	5,000
10/09/54	Maryland State	34	NC A&T	13	6,000
11/12/55	Virginia Union	7	West Virginia College	6	2,000
09/22/56	Maryland State	10	Virginia State	14	5,500
10/04/58	NC A&T	34	Virginia Union	6	5,000
09/23/78	Elizabeth City	27	Norfolk State	9	13,500
09/22/79	Norfolk State	18	Elizabeth City	6	12,000
09/28/80	Elizabeth City	21	Norfolk State	12	17,000
09/24/83	Elizabeth City	15	Norfolk State	0	21,500
09/22/84	Norfolk State	17	Elizabeth City	0	22,000
09/28/85	Norfolk State	45	Elizabeth City	3	17,000
09/25/86	Elizabeth City	20	Norfolk State	14	22,147
09/26/87	Norfolk State	26	Elizabeth City	7	22,500
09/26/88	Norfolk State	20	Elizabeth City	6	15,583
09/24/89	Norfolk State	37	Elizabeth City	0	7,089
09/22/90	Norfolk State	29	Elizabeth City	0	12,321
10/07/95	Norfolk State	35	Bethune-Cookman	33	8,716
09/28/96	Norfolk State	27	Delaware State	23	11,801

Appendix III

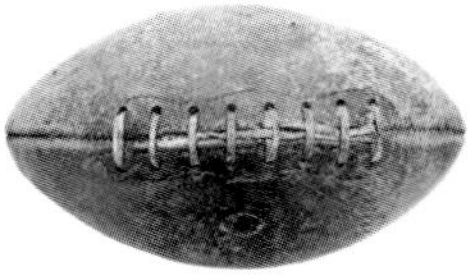

Norfolk State's Final Home Games

1996

DATE	TEAMS AND SCORES				ATTENDANCE
08/31	Norfolk State	15	Virginia State	24	28,758
09/15	Norfolk State	21	Livingstone	20	11,643
09/28	Norfolk State	27	Delaware State	23	11,001
10/05	Norfolk State	14	Central State	24	10,174
10/19	Norfolk State	33	Virginia Union	0	26,385

2009 Old Dominion University Football Roster (numerical)

No.	Name	Pos.	Class	Ht.	Wt.	Hometown/High School/Transfer
1	Ricky Nichols	DB	Fr.-r	5'11"	170	Norfolk, VA/Maury
2	Tommy Reamon	QB	Fr.-r	6'2"	220	Newport News, VA /Gloucester
3	Marquel Thomas	WR	Fr.	6'3"	175	VA Beach, VA/Bayside/ North Carolina Tech
4	Reid Evans	WR	Fr.-r	5'10"	170	Hampton, VA/Phoebus
5	Carlos Davis	WR	Fr.-r	5'10"	160	Ft. Washington, MD/Friendly
6	Alex Arain	WR	Fr.-r	6'4"	195	Virginia Beach, VA/Kempsville
7	Nick Mayers	WR	Fr.-r	5'7"	170	Virginia Beach, VA/Landstown
8	Marvin "Trey" Bryant	WR	Fr.-r	6'1"	215	Pikesville, MD/Pikesville Senior
9	Desmond Williams	WR	Fr.-r	5'11"	190	Windsor, NC/Bertie
10	Devon Simmons	DB	Fr.-r	6'2"	190	Newport News, VA/Denbigh
11	Bobby Cooper	QB	Fr.-r	6'3"	210	Davidsonville, MD/South River
12	Craig Wilkins	DB	Fr.-r	6'0"	200	Washington, D.C./H.D. Woodson
13	Marcus Lee	P	Fr.	6'1"	175	Wilmington, NC/Hoggard
14	Drew Hareza	K/P	Fr.-r	6'0"	205	McDonald, PA/South Fayette
15	Dan Pitts	QB	Fr.-r	6'5"	215	Virginia Beach, VA/Ocean Lakes
16	Fred Credle	WR	Fr.-r	5'11"	170	Chesapeake, VA/Deep Creek
17	Thomas DeMarco	QB	So.-r	5'11"	205	Palm Desert, CA /Palm Desert/ College of the Desert
18	Donald Smith	DB	Fr.-r	5'11"	170	Chesapeake, VA/Indian River
20	Jeremie Simmons	RB	Fr.-r	5'9"	210	Norfolk, VA /Lake Taylor
21	Tavon Gatlin	WR	Fr.	5'10"	170	VA Beach, VA/Green Run
22	T.J. Cowart	DB	Fr.-r	5'9"	180	Virginia Beach, VA/Ocean Lakes
24	A.T. Aoelua	DB	Jr.	5'8"	190	Pago, Pago, America Samoa/ Fagaitua/Monterey

No.	Name	Pos.	Class	Ht.	Wt.	Hometown/High School/Transfer
						Peninsula College
25	Mario Crawford	RB	Fr.	5'8"	165	Detroit, Mich./Romulus/ Fork Union Military Academy
23	Jamar Parham	RB	Fr.-r	5'7"	170	Chesterfield, VA/Matoaca
26	Josh Asare	DB	So.-r	5'10"	170	Woodbridge, VA/Potomac/ Shepherd University
27	Carvin Powell	DB	Fr.	6'3"	200	Chesapeake, VA/Great Bridge
28	Markell Wilkins	DB	Fr.	5'8"	160	Hampton, VA/Phoebus
29	Patrick Young	DB	Fr.	6'0"	185	VA Beach, VA/Green Run
30	Marquis Johnson	DB	Jr.	5'8"	165	San Diego, CA/Redlands East Valley/Santa Rosa JC
31	Jonathan Plisco	P	Fr.-r	6'0"	220	Newport News, VA/Woodside
32	C.J. Reaves	DB	Jr.-r	5'7"	175	Sterling, VA/ Dominion/Ferrum
33	Alex McLaughlin	RB	Jr.	5'8"	200	Burnsville, MN/Apple Valley/ Ridgewater College
34	J.J. Williams	LB	So.-r	6'2"	220	Derby, KS/Derby/Garden City CC
35	Xavier Duckett	LB	Fr.	6'0"	200	Roanoke, VA/Northside
36	Jake Sweedyk	LB	Jr.-r	6'3"	200	Walker, MI/West Catholic/ Grand Rapids CC
37	Gerald Anderson	LB	Jr.	6'2"	215	Winchester, VA/Handley
38	Benjamin Knerr	P	Fr.-r	6'1"	175	Chesapeake, VA/Indian River
40	B.J. McLaughlin	LB	Fr.-r	5'11"	205	Columbia, VA/Goochland
41	Daniel Brian	TE	Fr.-r	6'3"	205	Virginia Beach, VA/Kempsville
42	Brady Travers	K/P	Fr.	6'3"	190	Stafford, VA/Colonial Forge
43	John Michael Sparagna	FB	Fr.-r	6'0"	210	Mechanicsville, VA/Atlee
44	Mychael McJunkins	LB	Jr.	6'0"	230	Kansas City, KS/Washington/ Independence CC
45	Mateus Porter	LB	So.-r	6'1"	220	Pacifica, CA/Terra Nova/ College of San Mateo
46	John Darr	LB	Fr.	6'0"	215	Forestville, MD/Suitland

No.	Name	Pos.	Class	Ht.	Wt.	Hometown/High School/Transfer
47	Andrew Council	CB	So.-r	6'0"	185	Newport News, VA /Denbigh
48	Joe Cochrane	WR	Jr.-r	6'1"	205	Chesapeake, VA/Western Branch
49	Steven Schesventer	LS	Fr.-r	5'8"	200	Virginia Beach, VA/Salem
50	Dustin Phillips	LS	So.-r	6'0"	220	Woodland, CA/Woodland/Yuba CC
51	Michael Colbert	LB	Fr.-r	6'1"	205	Fayetteville, NC/E.E. Smith
52	Nikita Logan	LB	Fr.-r	5'10"	215	Danville, VA/George Washington
53	Devin Coleman	DE	Fr.-r	6'4"	235	Ashland, VA/Patrick Henry
54	Jeff Crawford	DL	Fr.-r	6'0"	300	Virginia Beach, VA/Green Run HS
55	Erik Saylor	DL	Fr.-r	6'2"	265	Ijamsville, MD/Urbana
56	Michael R. Williams	LB/DL	Fr.-r	6'2"	210	Norfolk, VA/Norview
57	Robbie Duncan	OL	Fr.-r	6'4"	280	Sterling, VA/Parkview
58	Jeremy Hensley	OL	So.-r	6'1"	285	La Palma, CA/Kennedy/ Fullerton College
59	Shantea Green	DE	Jr.	6'2"	240	Fort Myers, Fla./Lehigh/ Northland CC
61	Martin Petras	OL	Fr.	6'4"	260	Great Falls, VA/Langley
63	Charles Walls	OL	Fr.-r	6'2"	280	Virginia Beach, VA/Tallwood
65	Perry Owens	OL	Fr.	6'3"	275	Edenton, NC/John A. Holmes
66	Alex Bell	OL	Fr.	6'5"	260	Houston, DE/Milford
69	Blake Cornalino	OL	Jr.	6'2"	275	Upland, CA/Upland/ Mt. San Antonio College
70	Brandon Carr	OL	Fr.-r	6'2"	280	Chesapeake, VA/Western Branch/ Fork Union
71	Tobin Cameron	OL	So.-r	6'4"	275	Healdsburg, CA/Healdsburg/ Santa Rosa JC
72	Patrick McNichols	OL	Fr.	6'4"	285	Roaknoke, VA/Lord Botetourt
73	Jack Lowney	OL	Fr.	6'4"	260	Narberth, PA/Archbishop Carroll
75	Bryan Morrison	OL	Fr.-r	6'2"	270	Ashburn, VA/Broad Run
76	Ryan Jenson	OL	Jr.	6'4"	285	Petaluma, CA/Petaluma/ Santa Rosa JC

No.	Name	Pos.	Class	Ht.	Wt.	Hometown/High School/Transfer
77	Travis Peyton	OL	Fr.-r	6'4"	270	Woodbridge, VA/Forest Park
78	Justin Klingerman	OL	So.-r	6'3"	280	Valley Center, CA/Valley Center/ Palomar College
79	Logo Maluia	OL	Jr.-r	6'3"	295	Pacifica, CA/Terra Nova/ College of San Mateo
80	Michael E. Williams	WR	Fr.-r	5'10"	175	Manassas, VA/Forest Park
81	Daniel Harvey	WR	Jr.-r	6'0"	185	Bridgewater, VA/Turner Ashby/ James Madison
82	Monty Smalley	WR	Fr.	5'11"	160	Richmond, VA/Douglas Freeman
83	Kai Blanco	TE	Fr.-r	6'3"	230	Alexandria, VA/Mount Vernon
84	Dorian Jackson	WR	Fr.-r	5'10"	180	Colonial Heights, VA/Matoaca
85	Chris Lovitt	WR	Fr.-r	5'9"	190	Stafford, VA/Colonial Forge
88	Matt Carrillo	TE	Jr.-r	6'4"	250	La Mirada, CA/St. Paul/ Mt. San Antonio College
89	James Edwards	TE	So.-r	6'3"	230	Virginia Beach, VA/Landstown
90	Chris Burnette	DL	Fr.-r	6'4"	270	Randallstown, MD/Gilman School
91	Andrew Turner	DL	Fr.-r	6'3"	245	Virginia Beach, VA/Kellam
92	Tyler Damato	LB	Fr.-r	6'1"	220	Virginia Beach, VA/Landstown
93	Chad King	DL	So.-r	6'3"	250	Springfield, VA/Mount Vernon/ Ohio Dominican
94	Justin Hill	DL	So.-r	6'5"	250	Midlothian, VA/Manchester
95	Nate Barnes	DE	Fr.	6'5"	230	Newport News, VA/Heritage
96	Jason Fuller	DE	Sr.	6'5"	255	VA Beach, VA/Kempsville/Virginia
97	Edmon McClam	DL	So.-r	6'6"	260	Coward, SC/Lake City/ Louisburg College
98	Alex Johnson	DE	Fr.	6'3"	210	New Canton, VA/ Buckingham County/Fork Union
99	Andrew Slebonick	DL	Fr.-r	6'5"	230	Stafford, VA/North Stafford

Bibliography

ARCHIVAL COLLECTIONS

Three Scrapbooks 1930-1945

"Foreman Field" Folders, ODU Presidential Papers, Box 3, Lewis W. Webb, 1946-1951, Boxes 73, 84, and 148, James L. Bugg, Jr.; and Alfred B. Rollins, Box 16, Special Collections and University Archives, Patricia W. and J. Douglas Perry, ODU Libraries (used with permission)

Administrative Files, Norfolk Division, 1930-1941, Boxes 30-33

ODU Football History and Correspondence, Box X, Records of the College, RG-33, SG:5, Special Collections and University Archives, Patricia W. and J. Douglas Perry Library, Old Dominion University Libraries, Norfolk VA 23529

Photographs, Sargeant Memorial Room (Norfolk Municipal Library)

BOOKS AND ARTICLES

Brydges, Maggie, et al. *Old Dominion University: From the Great Depression to the New Millennium*, 1930-2000. Norfolk: Old Dominion University, 2000.

Raper, Jim. "ODU's Football Heritage: Norfolk Division Players Share Their Gridiron Memories," *ODU: A Magazine for Alumni and Friends* (Fall 2006): 8-10.

Rutyna, Richard A. and John W. Kuehl. *Old Dominion University: Heritage and Horizons*. Norfolk: The Donning Company Publishers, 1987.

Schmidt, Raymond. "American College Athletics: The 1929 Iowa Football Scandal: Paying Tribute to the Carnegie Report?" *Journal of Sport History* 34 (Fall 2007): 343-52;

Scribner, Robert. "Touchdown," *Virginia Cavalcade* 3 (Autumn 1954): 43-47.

Smith, Ron. "The William and Mary Athletic Scandal of 1951: Governance and the Battle for Academic and Athletic Integrity," *Journal of Sport History* 34 (Fall 2007): 353-88.

Sweeney, James R. *Old Dominion University: A Half Century of Service*. Norfolk: Old

Dominion University, 1980.

Walker, Carroll. Norfolk: A Pictorial History. Virginia Beach, VA: The Donning Company Publishers, 1975.

Watterson, John S. "The Death of Archer Christian: College Presidents and the Reform of College Football," *Journal of Sport History* 72 (Summer 1995): 149-67.

Watterson, John S. *College Football: History, Spectacle, Controversy*. Baltimore: The Johns Hopkins University Press, 2000.

Wilford, Kale, Bob Moskowitz and Charles M. Hollaway. *Goal to Goal:100 Seasons of Football at William and Mary*. Williamsburg; Botetourt Press, 1997.

INTERVIEWS

Baker, William with Tom Garrett, 23 June 2009

Brichter, Joe with Peter Stewart (telephone), 4 June 2009

Brown, John with Tom Garrett and Peter Stewart, 27 May 2009

Walker, Rhea with Tom Garrett, Peter Stewart and Troy Valos, 18 May 2009

Whitehurst, G. William with Peter Stewart, 19 June 2009

MUNICIPAL RECORDS (microfilm)

Norfolk. City Records Book. Council Minutes, 3 September 1935

NEWSPAPERS (microfilm)

The Flat Hat (College of William and Mary), 1930-1939

The High Hat (Norfolk Division of the College of William and Mary and Virginia Tech), 1931-1941

Norfolk Journal and Guide, 1938-1970

Mace and Crown (Old Dominion University), 1980-1990

Miami Herald, 1932

Norfolk Virginian, 1890-1898

The Virginian-Pilot (Norfolk), 1899-2009

Norfolk Ledger-Dispatch, 1930-1941

Old Gold and Black (Wake Forest University), 1932

YEARBOOKS

The Commodore (Maury High School), Vols. 20-32, 1928-1939

Endnotes

CHAPTER I

1. *Norfolk Virginian*, 22 and 30 October and 12 November 1893; 15 October 1896; *The Virginian-Pilot*, 28 October 1900 and 13 October 1901.
2. *The Virginian-Pilot*, 24 November 1900.
3. *The Virginian-Pilot*, 18, 24 and 25 November 1900.
4. *The Virginian-Pilot*, 23-26 November 1901.
5. *The Virginian-Pilot*, 9-19 November 1902.
6. *The Virginian-Pilot*, 19-28 November 1902.
7. *The Virginian-Pilot*, 7, 24, and 31 October and 21 November 1903.
8. *The Virginian-Pilot*, 4 and 25 November and 1 December 1905
9. Robert Scribner, "Touchdown," *Virginia Cavalcade* 3 (Autumn 1954): 43-47; *The Virginian-Pilot*, 6 November 1904.
10. John S. Watterson, *College Football: History, Spectacle, Controversy* (Baltimore: Johns Hopkins University Press, 2000), pp. 99-119.
11. *The Virginian-Pilot*, 26 August 1912; and John S. Watterson, "The Death of Archer Christian: College Presidents and the Reform of College Football," *Journal of Sport History* 72 (Summer 1995): 149-67.
12. *The Virginian-Pilot*, 3, 4, 10, 11, 29, and 30 November 1906.
13. *The Virginian-Pilot*, 3 and 29 November 1907, 27 November 1908, 25 and 26 November 1909, 13 November 1910.
14. *The Virginian-Pilot*, 30 November and 1 December 1911, and 29 November 1912, 28 November 1913.
15. *The Virginian-Pilot*, 7 November 1914 and 20 November 1915.
16. *The Virginian-Pilot*, 30 November 1916 and 28 November-1 December 1917.
17. *The Virginian-Pilot*, 12 November 1920, 4 November 1923, 6 November 1924, 27 October 1925.

18. *The Virginian-Pilot*, 17 October 1926, 3 November 1927, 4 November 1928, and 15 October 1930.
19. The Virginian-Pilot, 7 November 1915; and Carroll Walker, *Norfolk: A Pictorial History* (Virginia Beach, VA: The Donning Company Publishers, 1975), pp. 158-59.
20. *The Virginian-Pilot*, 26 November 1920.
21. *The Virginian-Pilot*, 22 November and 18 December 1921.
22. *The Virginian-Pilot*, 5 December 1926, 7 November 1927, and 4 December 1938.
23. *The Virginian-Pilot*, 7 November 1927 and 4 November 1928.

CHAPTER II

1. *The Virginian-Pilot*t, 9 July 1930 and 3, 4, and 14 September 1930; also *The Ledger-Dispatch*, 4, 9, and 13 September.
2. Watterson, College Football, pp. 165-76; Raymond Schmidt, "American College Athletics: The 1929 Iowa Football Scandal: Paying Tribute to the Carnegie Report?" *Journal of Sport History* 34 (Fall 2007): 343-52.
3. *The Ledger-Dispatch*, 12 September 1930.
4. *The Virginian-Pilot*, 27 September 1930.
5. *The Virginian-Pilot*, 4 October 1930; and *The Ledger-Dispatch*, 20 September and 3 October 1930.
6. *The Ledger-Dispatch*, 11 October 1930.
7. *The Virginian-Pilot* and *The Ledger-Dispatch*, 16 October 1930; and *The Flat Hat*, 7 November 1930.
8. *The Virginian-Pilot*, 24 and 25 October 1930.
9. *The Virginian-Pilot*, 30 October and 1 November 1930; and *The Flat Hat*, 7 November 1930.
10. *The Virginian-Pilot*, 10, 11, 18, 25 October and 1, 8, 12, 15, 19 and 23 November 1930.
11. *The High Hat*, 23 January 1931.
12. *The Virginian-Pilot*, 18, 19, and 23 September 1931.
13. *The Virginian-Pilot*, 4 October 1931.
14. *The High Hat*, 2 October 1931.
15. *The Virginian-Pilot*, 11 October 1931.

16. *The High Hat*, 23 October 1931.
17. *The Virginian-Pilot*, 17 October 1931; High Hat, 23 October 1931; and *The Flat Hat*, 27 October 1931.
18. *The High Hat*, 9 October 1931.
19. *The High Hat*, 6 November 1931.
20. *The Virginian-Pilot*, 9-12 November 1931; and *The Ledger-Dispatch*, 9 November 1931.
21. *The Virginian-Pilot*, 21-22 November 1931.
22. *The High Hat*, 4 December 1931.
23. *The Virginian-Pilot*, 6 December 1931.
24. *The Virginian-Pilot*, 9 and 20 September 1932.
25. *The Virginian-Pilot*, 17 and 28 September 1932.
26. *The Virginian-Pilot*, 1 October 1932; and *The Flat Hat*, 4 October 1932.
27. *The Virginian-Pilot*, 8 October 1932; and *Old Gold and Black*, 15 October 1932.
28. *The Virginian-Pilot*, 7 September and 11-15 October 1932.
29. *The Virginian-Pilot*, 30 November 1947.
30. Walker interview, 18 May 2009.
31. *Miami Herald*, 18 September and 9-15 October 1932.
32. *The High Hat*, 28 October 1932; *The Virginian-Pilot*, 23 October 1932..
33. *The Virginian-Pilot*, 5 November 1932.
34. *The Virginian-Pilot*, 29-30 October 1932.
35. *The Virginian-Pilot*, 11 and 20 November 1932.
36. *The High Hat*, 11 November 1932, 1 January and 24 February 1933.

CHAPTER III

1. *The Virginian-Pilot*, 10, 15, 18 and 22 September 1933; and *The High Hat*, 30 September 1933.
2. *The Flat Hat*, 10 October 1933.
3. *The High Hat*, 30 September 1933; and *The Virginian-Pilot*, 4, 7, 8, 14, and 15 October 1933.
4. *The Virginian-Pilot*, 19-21 October 1933; and Walker interview, 18 May 2009.
5. *The Ledger-Dispatch*, 27-28 October 1933.

6. Walker interview, 18 May 2009.
7. *The Virginian-Pilot*, 27-28 October 1933.
8. *The Virginian-Pilot*, 9-11 November 1933.
9. *The Virginian-Pilot*, 18 November 1933.
10. *The Virginian-Pilot*, 24-25 November 1933.
11. *The High Hat*, 4 December, 1933 and Folder #7 (Athletics: Tommy Scott, 1932-39), Box 30, Administrative Files, Norfolk Division, Special Collections and University Archives, Patricia W. and J. Douglas Perry Library, Old Dominion University Libraries, Norfolk, VA 23529 (hereafter ODU Archives).
12. *The Virginian-Pilot*, 2, 5, and 6 October 1934. The Division played its home games that year at Larchmont Field, the current site of the Williamsburg Lawn. Scott may have opted to play fewer games at Bain Field because its owners had raised the rental rate from 10 percent of the gate receipts to 20 percent.
13. *The Virginian-Pilot*, 11 October 1934.
14. *The Virginian-Pilot*, 16 and 20 October 1934; and Walker interview, 18 May 2009.
15. *The Virginian-Pilot*, 2 and 3 November; and *The Ledger-Dispatch*, 3 November 1934.
16. *The Virginian-Pilot*, 10 November 1934; and *The Flat Hat*, 13 November 1934.
17. *The Virginian-Pilot*, 23-24 November 1934; and Walker interview, 18 May 2009.
18. *The Virginian-Pilot*, 28 September 1935.
19. *The Virginian-Pilot*, 6 October 1935.
20. *The Virginian-Pilot*, 13 October 1935.
21. *The Virginian-Pilot*, 25 October 1935.
22. *The Virginian-Pilot*, 25-27 October 1935.
23. *The Virginian-Pilot*, 2-3 November 1935; and *The High Hat*, 12 November 1935.
24. *The Virginian-Pilot*, 13 and 16 November 1935.
25. *The Virginian-Pilot*, 21 and 23 November 1935.
26. *The Virginian-Pilot*, 8 December 1935.
27. *The High Hat*, 13 December 1935 and 9 January 1937.
28. *The High Hat*, 8 March and 1 November 1935.
29. *The High Hat*, 11 October 1935; and Watterson, College Football, p. 201.

CHAPTER IV

1. *The Virginian-Pilot*, 29 December 1933 and 3 January 1934.
2. Norfolk City Council Resolution, 3 September 1935, City Records Book (microfilm) and James R. Sweeney, *Old Dominion University: A Half Century of Service* (Norfolk: Old Dominion University, 1980), pp. 14-16.
3. Undated clippings in Scrapbook, 1930-1940, ODU Archives; and *The Virginian-Pilot* 6 June 1937.
4. *The Ledger-Dispatch*, 3 November 1934; and *The Virginian-Pilot*, 26 June 1935.
5. Walker interview, 18 May 2009.
6. *The Virginian-Pilot*, 19 September 1936.
7. *The Virginian-Pilot*, 7 September, 2 and 13 October 1936, and 4 April 1937.
8. *The Virginian-Pilot*, 4 October 1936.
9. *The Virginian-Pilot*, 8 August 1938.
10. *The Ledger-Dispatch*, 21 October 1939.
11. Scrapbook, 1930-1940, p. 72, ODU Archives.
12. *The Virginian-Pilot*, 20-22 September 1940; *The Ledger-Dispatch*, 10 October 1940.
13. *The High Hat*, 8 February 1935.

CHAPTER V

1. *The Virginian-Pilot*, 24 September and 2 October 1936.
2. *The Virginian-Pilot*, 3, 9 and 13 October 1936.
3. *The High Hat*, 16 October 1936.
4. *The Virginian-Pilot*, 17 and 18 October 1936.
5. *The Virginian-Pilot*, 24 October 1936.
6. *The Virginian-Pilot*, 1 November 1936.
7. *The Virginian-Pilot*, 6 November 1936.
8. *The Virginian-Pilot*, 12 November 1936.
9. *The High Hat*, 1 December 1936.
10. *The Virginian-Pilot*, 25 September 1937.

11. *The Virginian-Pilot*, 29-30 September and 1-2 October 1937.
12. *The Virginian-Pilot*, 9 October 1937.
13. *The Virginian-Pilot*, 14-16 October 1937.
14. *The Virginian-Pilot*, 23-24 October 1937.
15. *The Virginian-Pilot*, 30 October 1937.
16. *The Virginian-Pilot*, 5 and 6 November 1937; and *The Flat Hat*, 9 November 1937.
17. *The Virginian-Pilot*, 14-15 November 1937.
18. *The Virginian-Pilot*, 19-21 November 1937.
19. *The High Hat*, 23 September 1938.
20. *The High Hat*, 23 September 1938.
21. *The Virginian-Pilot*, 25 September 1937; and *The High Hat*, 30 September 1938.
22. *The Virginian-Pilot*, 29 September and 1 October 1938.
23. *The Virginian-Pilot*, 7-8 October 1938.
24. *The Virginian-Pilot*, 14-16 October 1938.
25. *The Virginian-Pilot*, 23 October 1938; and Brichter interview, 4 June 2009.
26. *The Virginian-Pilot*, 28-30 October 1938 and 15 November 1981, D14; and Brown interview, 27 May 2009.
27. *The Virginian-Pilot*, 4-5 November 1938; and *The Flat Hat*, 5 November 1938.
28. *The Virginian-Pilot*, 12 November 1938.

CHAPTER VI

1. *The High Hat*, 20 September 1939.
2. *The Virginian-Pilot*, 25 September 1939.
3. Baker interview, 23 June 2009.
4. *The Virginian-Pilot*, 25 September 1939.
5. *The Virginian-Pilot*, 29 and 30 September 1939.
6. *The Virginian-Pilot*, 7 and 15 October 1939.
7. *The Virginian-Pilot*, 21 October 1939.
8. *The Virginian-Pilot*, 29 October 1939; High Hat, 3 November 1939;

and Bakerinterview, 23 June 2009.

9. *The Virginian-Pilot*, 3-5 November 1939.

10. *The High Hat*, 17 November 1939.

11. *The Virginian-Pilot*, 18 November 1939.

12. *The Virginian-Pilot*, 25 November 1939; and Brown interview, 27 May 2009.

13. *The Flat Hat*, 28 November 1939.

14. W.T. Hodges to Carl Voyles, 27 July 1939 (carbon), Box 31, Folder IV, Administrative Files, ODU Archives; Brichter interview, 4 June 2009; and Baker interview, 23 June 2009.

15. Copy of letter, 8 February 1940, Cox to Carlyle Shepard, Box 33, Administrative Files, ODU Archives.

16. *The Virginian-Pilot,* 3 September and 4 October 1940.

17. *The Virginian-Pilot*, 9-13 October 1940.

18. *The Virginian-Pilot*, 18 October 1940.

19. *The Virginian-Pilot*, 18 October and 17-19 November 1940.

20. *The High Hat*, 1 November 1940.

21. *The Virginian-Pilot*, 8 November 1940.

22. *The Virginian-Pilot*, 4-9 November 1940; and Invoices, Folder 9, Administrative Files, 1940 ODU Archives.

23. *The Virginian-Pilot*, 17 November 1940.

24. *The Virginian-Pilot*, 22 November 1940.

25. *The Virginian-Pilot*, 2 February 1941.

26. *The High Hat*, 29 February and 24 May 1941.

27. Undated clipping in Scrapbook, 1941, p. 1, ODU Archives.

28. *The Virginian-Pilot*, 3 August 1941.

29. *The Virginian-Pilot*, 19 September 1940.

30. *The Ledger-Dispatch*, 11 March 1941; and Whitehurst interview, 19 June 2009.

31. *The Ledger-Dispatch*, 12 March 1941; *The Virginian-Pilot* (Compass), "From the Gridiron to War, ODU Honors Its 'Living Legends,'" 24 May 2009, pp. 1, 10; *The Virginian-Pilot*, 15 November 1981, D14; and Brichter interview, 4 June 2009.

32. Scrapbook, 1941-1945, ODU Archives.

CHAPTER VII

1. *The Virginian-Pilot*, 2 January 1941 and 12 November 1948.
2. *The Virginian-Pilot*, 12-17 October 1941.
3. *The Virginian-Pilot*, 15 December 1941.
4. *The Virginian-Pilot*, 1 and 15 November 1942.
5. *The Virginian-Pilot*, 18 November 1945 and 8 December 1946; and Scrapbook, 1930-1940, p. 82, ODU Archives.
6. Letters 29 June 1953 and 5 and 15 March, 1957, "Foreman Athletic Field," 1957 Correspondence, Box X, Records of the College and Folder 11, "Foreman Field," Presidential Papers of Lewis W. Webb, 1946-1951, Box 3, Special Collections, ODU Archives.
7. *The Virginian-Pilot*, 15-16 September 1946.
8. *The Virginian-Pilot*, 19 November 1945.
9. *The Virginian-Pilot*, 7 November 1949, 1 November 1954, 28 October 1957, and 8 November 1958.
10. *The Virginian-Pilot*, 9 October 1948.
11. *The Virginian-Pilot*, September-November 1958.
12. *Norfolk Journal and Guide*, 24 October 1953.
13. *The Virginian-Pilot*, 17 November 1974.
14. *The Virginian-Pilot*, 22 October 1978.
15. *The Virginian-Pilot*, 22 February 1996.
16. *The Virginian-Pilot*, 2-10 October 1954, 2 November 1958, 20 September 1959, and 27 September 1960.
17. *The Virginian-Pilot*, 29 August and 5 September 1965, 21 August 1966, and 16 and 23 August 1971.
18. *The Virginian-Pilot*, 11 November 1973, 15, 22 and 29 September, 6, 13, 20, 27 October, 17 November, and 22 December 1974.
19. *The Virginian-Pilot*, 22 October 1976, and 5 November 1976 Compass.
20. *The Virginian-Pilot*, 12 October 1988; "Demolition of Foreman Field" Folder, Series II, Box 73 Folder 14, Series III, Box 148, Office of the President, James L. Bugg Jr.; and "Foreman Field" Folder, ODU Archives; and *The Virginian-Pilot*, 26 October 1975.

21. "Foreman Field" Folder, Box 16, Presidential Papers of Alfred B. Rollins, ODU Archives.
22. *The Virginian-Pilot*, 18 October 1982, 20 September 1984, 20 October 1985.
23. *The Virginian-Pilot*, 21 October 1990.
24. *The Virginian-Pilot*, 20 October 1996.
25. *The Virginian-Pilot*, 5 November 1995, C1 and 12.

CHAPTER VIII

1. *The Virginian-Pilot*, 12, 16, 19 August, 9 and 20 September 1951; and Ron Smith, "The William and Mary Athletic Scandal of 1951: Governance and the Battle for Academic and Athletic Integrity," *Journal of Sport History* 34 (Fall 2007): 353-88.
2. *The Virginian-Pilot*, 2 December 1960.
3. *The Virginian-Pilot*, 3 November 1970.
4. *ODU Mace and Crown*, 9 September 1982.
5. *ODU Mace and Crown*, 12 December 1982 and 17 January 1983.
6. *ODU Mace and Crown*, 3 October 1983.
7. *The Virginian-Pilot*, 16 October 1983.
8. *The Virginian-Pilot*, 7 October 1984.
9. *The Virginian-Pilot*, 11 April 1985; and *ODU Mace and Crown*, 17 October 1985.
10. *ODU Mace and Crown*, 29 January 1987.
11. *The Virginian-Pilot*, 5 and 6 November 1988.
12. *The Virginian-Pilot*, 26 January, 24 and 28 April, 1 and 12 May, 12, 14, 16, 18, 22, and 25 June, 25 August, 22 October, and 11 and 17 December 2005; 21 April, 28 and 31 May, 1 June, 8 and 13 September (two articles), 3 and 24 October, and 4 November 2006, and 24 January, and 2, 6, 9, and 12 February 2007.